ABOUT T

Kay White, *Smart Career* ___ *...entor for Corporate Career Women,* coaches and mentors ambitious career women to maximise their skills, experience and wisdom by leveraging their opportunities at a time when there's never been a better time to be a corporate woman putting her foot down in her career. She is the founder of mentoring & training company *Way Forward Solutions Ltd (2006)* and also author of the #1 bestseller *The A to Z of Being Understood (2011).* Her client and voluntary work focusses on continual career success strategies for women who want to future-proof their careers and be rewarded and recognised for the value they add, all without losing themselves or selling their souls in the process.

Kay lives in the UK in the Essex countryside with her husband Snowy and their 3 rescue hounds, Pharaoh, DeeDee & Jeffrey.

kaywhite.com
alwaysyourmove.com
Facebook.com/kayjwhite
@kayjwhite

IT'S *ALWAYS* **YOUR MOVE**

It's *Always* Your Move

Purposeful Progress for Corporate Career Women

Copyright © 2018 by Kay White
www.kaywhite.com

ISBN-13: 978-0-9964460-9-9
ISBN-10: 0-9964460-9-5

Published by: Expert Author Publishing
http://expertauthorpublishing.com

Canadian Address:
1108 - 1155 The High Street,
Coquitlam, BC, Canada V3B.7W4
Phone: (604) 941-3041
Fax: (604) 944-7993

US Address
1300 Boblett Street
Unit A-218
Blaine, WA 98230
Phone: (866) 492-6623
Fax: (250) 493-6603

Cover design and layout: Skyward Ink Ltd., USA
Back cover photo: Steve Cozart Photography

We women *can* have it all – just not all at the same time or on the same day.

Dedicated to you, a woman like me, who's perfectly imperfect and committed to doing her best.

Remember, it's *always* your move.

FOREWORD

It's _Always_ Your Move is designed to be a light to shine on your career path when sometimes it's too dark or confusing to see the way ahead.

The stories of women who, just like you, took time to plot, plan and work out how and where they wanted their careers to go are all true. Some of their names may have been changed for their client privacy but their messages are included to reassure you about taking that next step and driving your own career bus.

Magic happens when you do.

FURTHER INSPIRATION FROM INSPIRATIONAL PEOPLE

"In her inimitable way, Kay White provides career guidance you can really use and she does it with intelligence, humour, and heart. Real-time examples, tangible tools and tips, and tons of encouragement along the way make this book the one that will coach you to your next career move – and the one after that."

Dr. Lois Frankel, author of the New York Times and Wall Street Journal bestselling business bible for women, *Nice Girls Don't Get the Corner Office*

"Everyone's career path is so different – for me it was never mapped out, and there was certainly no magic formula to get me where I am today. Having the courage to take on challenges, trust in my ability, and realise my value all played an important part in shaping my career, particularly when things got tough. But there was a time when I didn't have self-confidence, self-trust or know my value, and I learnt some tough lessons as a result.

This book, filled with Kay White's advice, strategies and principles for success, would have been a big help. It provides the insight and tools to help people as they progress through their career – a practical guidebook to help you confidently and strategically navigate the twists and turns and the ups and downs of your unique career journey."

Dame Inga Beale, CEO Lloyd's of London

"Kay White's book is an absolute must-read for anyone wishing to progress their career. Packed to the brim with real-life stories, tips for success, tools and resources, you cannot fail to take something away. If you are a woman who really wants to grab her career by the horns, then this book is definitely for you. I wish both Kay and her books were around at the start of my career! 100% recommended."

Vanessa Vallely OBE, Founder & Managing Director, *WeAreTheCity*

"Filled with straightforward, practical and immediately implementable strategies & tactics to support you on your journey onwards through the corporate maze. With this book Kay White offers a guiding light to illuminate your way forward. Role models are thin on the ground for women in the corporate world, especially peer group role models. This book offers straightforward, sound advice backed by real-life examples from women you can easily identify with, who have put Kay's guidance and experience into practice and boosted their confidence and their bank balance."

Fiona Lane, Head of Strategy, International Insurance Broker

"This book is a must-read for you if you know you can do so much more with your career than you're currently doing. Let Kay White's proven guidance, strategies and stories be your torch when sometimes it's too murky to see where you're going, and everything she offers

you works and comes from her experience and her heart. Put yourself in the driving seat of your career."
Chelsea Berler, Founder of Solamar Marketing Agency & Author, The Curious One

"It's great to read a book written by a woman who has walked her own corporate journey and who wants to make it easier for other women on their own journeys. Her real-life experiences and stories of her many clients capture the challenges *and* opportunities of the daily treadmill, the moments of fear that sometimes cripple you from taking the next steps and the humorous, down-to-earth style she uses to make her point. Kay encourages you to take those next steps and make them work for you – it's as if she's speaking directly to you which, I think, she really is. This book is a guide for any woman at any stage of her career and Kay certainly knows how to dress! An inspirational, tactical read."
Heather Melville OBE, Head of Business & Financial Inclusion, Corp & Private Banking, Nat West

Who amongst us has not felt a bit stuck in corporate life? When I saw the Contents Page of Kay White's latest book **It's** *Always* **Your Move** I knew I was going to find her straight-talking comments informative, relevant and witty. The introduction, just as in a good thriller novel, had me hooked. The phrase getting unstuck is a choice, the quotes throughout the book, the clear strategies she recommends and the myriad of stories about real women

in real situations resonated with me. Kay articulates many truths about being corporate career women and at the end of the book I guarantee that you'll be inspired to take action in your career and you'll want to share it with a friend."
Dr Maggie Semple, OBE, FCGI. Founder of The Semple Group

"This is a book I wish I had when I was beginning my career. While I always knew that it was my move, sometimes I lacked the courage and often the pragmatic career skills to navigate through the intense advertising industry. Kay White's book is an inspirational blueprint on how to strategically move through your career with grace, savvy, and discipline. Her principles combined with real-life stories pack a powerful 1-2 punch. Quite simply, she is a Firestarter and her book will ignite, fuel and accelerate the careers of women no matter where they live or what stage they're at."
Kathy Palokoff, author of Firestarters: How Innovators, Instigators, and Initiators Can Inspire You to Ignite Your Own Life.

"For so many women treading water in the corporate oceans there is a nagging feeling that is difficult to define. You can feel stuck and if you just knew the questions to ask you could search for the answers and get your career back on track. In her latest book Kay White has covered both sides of the equation. In her smart, simplistic, succinct (but honest and entertaining) manner she has brilliantly laid out priceless career success guidance for you and provided answers to empower you and make your career moving forward a given.

A must-read for the career woman who wants to make smart, considered and strategic moves throughout her career – without losing herself in the process." **Thomas M. Sterner** Author of "The Practicing Mind" and "Fully Engaged"

"I feel like I've come to the party regarding the value of networking, spending time focussing on career path and skills, and how important personal branding is, pretty late.

Kay's book, and also meeting Kay and attending her events, has helped me play catch-up big-time. It is a focussed, practical book, a guide really, and has helped me really understand the steps I needed to take to move my career to the next level. You can take the book in its entirety and then dip back in for those moments when you need to apply some planning and thought regarding a particular move or action.

Of the myriad of things the book's taught me, a key is taking control of my future in a way that's true to me - and finding your own way to be successful without, as Kay says, 'losing yourself'." **Karen Graves** EMEA Hub COO and Inclusion Advocate, International Insurance

CONTENTS

"The road to success
is *always* under
construction."

– LILY TOMLIN

PICK A PLACE TO START – BUT ALWAYS PICK YOURSELF

Your career is like a bus. A big red London bus if you will. You can either be up at the front in the driver's seat with responsibility for the controls and the direction it takes, or you can be a passenger. Most of the time, it's up to you to drive your own career bus.

Why should anyone else be more interested and invested in your own career success and satisfaction than you? We know deep down they're not, yet it's so easy to hand over the steering wheel. Somehow, it feels safer. Often, we have blind faith that others know better, have our best interests at heart or must give us permission to act or step up. Most of the time though, it's because we don't trust ourselves to take charge of our own destiny. We don't trust that *we* know best. We choose to back and believe in others, rather than to pick ourselves to believe in.

The 8 Principles of Your Career Success Cycle™ enables you to find yourself right where you are now and then use the strategies, ideas and stories to always find the confidence, certainty and belief in yourself to drive your own career. These 8 Principles will help you get unstuck.

You know, getting stuck can creep up on you and catch you unawares, but remaining stuck is a choice. When I started writing this book, we were on holiday with the sun shining and the water glistening bright blue. It was January, and we had escaped winter in London. I made the choice to start writing. I stopped fiddling about telling myself I didn't feel like it and procrastinating because I knew no one could write this book for me. Only I could.

So you see, I chose to drive my own bus and believe in *me*. I chose to get unstuck. Just like you, I believed I was up for the job.

Here are the 8 Principles we will cover in this book:

- o **Principle 1:** Embrace Your Expansion Tree
- o **Principle 2:** Discover What's Out There
- o **Principle 3:** Prepare, Plot, Plan (and Keep On Going)
- o **Principle 4:** Leverage Your Connections
- o **Principle 5:** Shine in Interviews and Appraisals
- o **Principle 6:** Negotiate More for Yourself
- o **Principle 7:** Accept and Move On with Grace and Gratitude
- o **Principle 8:** Navigate the First 100 Days and Beyond Success Route

HOW (AND WHY) I KNOW A THING OR TWO

I can remember the exact moment – the fork in the road if you will – when I knew I *had* to do something. Something else. Working as I had in London for over 20 years for one of top three global insurance brokers, I'd progressed from being an enthusiastic secretary at 18 years old to a divisional director in one of the most successful divisions of the company.

Deciding to switch from the non-business side of things to the 'sharp end' of broking global property risks had been quite a ride. I'd gone from being fairly carefree and relaxed about my working day to being in a highly demanding role, which stretched me both mentally and physically.

Just before I moved to the broking side, I felt like I was spinning my wheels and just going through the motions every day. It's soul destroying isn't it? If you take pride in what you do and know you're capable of so much more, just showing up and waiting for the time you can leave for home eats away at you. Hence, I decided to 'get my hands dirty'- as my dear father referred to it – when I moved over on to the broking side.

The learning curve was steep, and the rewards and demands were high. Long hours, big personalities with short tempers, early morning meetings and long lunches, business trips with weekend working, cancelling social events and gym classes and an expectation that you worked hard first before you had any chance of playing hard. I loved it. For a good few years, I loved it. Until I didn't.

As the constant pressure started to wear me down and the personalities I'd thought were so inspiring started to really grate on my nerves and well-being, I knew I was stuck. Frustrated, bad-tempered, bored and stuck.

The pivotal point happened one morning at about 7.30am when I arrived at the office. A couple of our team members were by the desk of my colleague, Martin, who hadn't yet arrived. Martin was going to be 40 years old that day and they were tying balloons with 'The Big 40' written on them on to the back of his chair.

I looked at those helium balloons bobbing about above the desk and could feel my pulse racing and my head screaming. "You can't be sitting here in three years when you're about to be 40, feeling like this, behaving like this and wanting to scream. You've got to do something."

That feeling of frustration was palpable – the sense of being trapped with the golden handcuffs of the title, a chunky salary, company car, pension, health insurance and all the things I thought were so key to my identity.

That moment was a defining one. We all have them one way or another, when you snap internally or out loud. That moment stuck with me, even though I wished Martin a happy birthday and went about my business that day, I knew something was about to happen and if *I* didn't make it happen then it would happen *to me*. I'd either make a decision or be called out for my behaviour and perceived lack of commitment. I made a decision.

I made my move after working out how much money my three months' notice period would generate, looking at my personal savings and long-term endowment policy that I could cash in and having a full and frank conversation with Snowy, my husband of just over two months.

I resigned within two weeks of the 'balloon moment'. I said things like "I just can't do this anymore. I'm bored and frustrated, and have worked since I was 18 years old." Something petulant and non-negotiable like that. It wasn't my finest hour, but it was me being backed against a wall thinking I didn't have any other option but to pull the plug.

The change I made has ultimately worked out for me. I now run a multiple six-figure mentoring and training company, Way Forward Solutions Limited. We are able to have three rescue hounds and I walk them every morning in the woods, when I previously would have been commuting.

I start my day working with career women – mainly on the telephone from my home office – plotting and planning with them their best moves in their own careers. I make time to go to the gym two or three times a week and I'm learning to play the drums.

It hasn't been a straight line though. I've worked part-time for a charity, studied, invested a lot of time and money in courses, (some were more productive than others) and, at times, looked at re-joining the corporate world. Running your own business is as inspiring and challenging as it is scary, frustrating and, sometimes, lonely.

I don't want you to do exactly what I did, now that I know much better. Now I understand about the various options I had, which I just couldn't see back then – the options which you might not be able to see either.

I want to share a retrospective insight with you. If I'd been more strategic about positioning my skills and experience and more careful about what I said about how I felt and who I said it to *before* I resigned, I would have given myself more options. I could have negotiated a move either internally or within the industry, which would have given me the fresh start I needed.

If I had been conscious of what I now know and had followed the steps within *The 8 Principles of Your Career Success Cycle*™, it would have been a more strategic rather than emotional decision. That's what I want for you. The ability to understand just how many options you have and to be more strategic about using them. When, and if, you're ready.

THIS BOOK IS FOR YOU IF...

So, in order to get the most out of this book, you need to understand if or where you are stuck or sense a change is needed and get to the source of the reason.

Here are the kind of statements that my myriad of clients have said to me as they were trying to figure out the source of their dissatisfaction and get unstuck. I suggest that you think about which of these statements may apply to you.

You will definitively know that *The 8 Principles of Your Career Success Cycle*™ are for you if...

o You underestimate the choices and skills you have and feel truly stuck.

o You are a woman returning to work from maternity leave and are unsure about your skills.

o You've been trying to secure a promotion and keep getting pushed back.

o You're sick and tired of being sick and tired, overworked and undervalued

o You watch others around you get offered the opportunities you know you're ready for.

o You sense that you're bored or restless but have lost the confidence to act.

o You feel queasy or uneasy at the thought of talking about yourself in interviews.

o You're happy enough with what you're doing but know you're underpaid.

o You fight in everyone else's corner for pay and opportunities but hate doing this for yourself.

o You're drawn to the idea of changing companies or departments but don't want to let anyone down.

- You don't have a clue about how to talk about yourself and your achievements.

- You can't see a natural next step but can't imagine staying as you are for another year.

- You have a boss who takes you for granted and doesn't think you'll ever leave.

- You sense you're not going to get offered a promotion opportunity and hate to be pushy.

- You've just moved roles but are overwhelmed with knowing all you don't know.

- You've just resigned and are fretting about how to talk about why and where you're going.

- You've been to see agency after agency and can't face the process any more so you may give up.

- You'd rather not negotiate about your salary so you just put up with what you get.

- You believe everyone else is more qualified or experienced than you and fear being found out.

- You just can't imagine having the time or energy to find another role so you put up and shut up.

- You've stayed where you are, trusting all will come out good and now feel you've missed the boat.

○ You've lost track of how many management restructures you've experienced and feel a little lost.

○ Your boss has changed so many times you know your experience and value have got lost in the cracks.

○ You moved roles and now, with the benefit of time, see how 'broken' things are.

○ You took a new role, and you've been offered another role – too soon.

○ You've been approached to speak to an agency or connection but dread speaking about yourself.

○ You don't have a CV or resumé and you have no idea how to put yourself across on paper.

○ You've gone for a new role, not secured it and now feel unsure or disheartened.

○ You find it all a bit confusing and stressful; you feel you're best off where you are quietly getting on with things.

HOW TO GET THE MOST OUT OF THIS BOOK

We as women, in my experience, like to read instructions and follow them. We like to have a place to find ourselves. This is what this book is about.

Having been asked "Kay, where do I start? I just don't know where to begin." or "I'm so scared about being interviewed again; I'd rather stay put" by so many brilliant and underestimated women, I knew I had to put finger to keyboard and dare myself to write this book.

I draw inspiration from many clients throughout this book and, naturally, from my own career path. Please read their stories and mine. Stories about others are one of the most powerful learning tools because they represent a mirror, which we can look at and see parts of ourselves.

I've also found many quotes, mainly from inspiring women, which I share with you here. They do, I believe, reiterate what the message is for us and I'm grateful for their counsel and wisdom.

I encourage you to read the whole book as I lead you through it. There are so many gems and insights from the stories of clients who've generously shared their results, successes, insights and lessons as they used *The 8 Principles of Your Career Success Cycle*™ to navigate their career path. Read it all because I wouldn't want you to miss a trick.

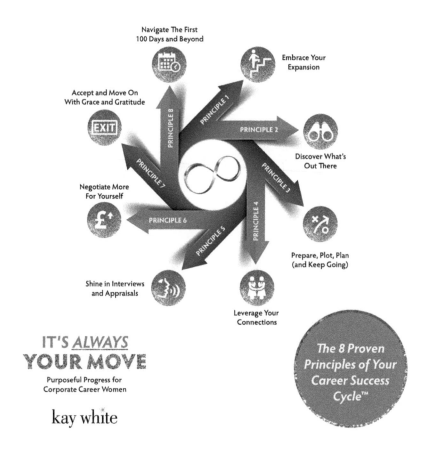

Navigate The First
100 Days and Beyond

Embrace Your
Expansion

Accept and Move On
With Grace and Gratitude

Discover What's
Out There

Negotiate More
For Yourself

Prepare, Plot, Plan
(and Keep Going)

Shine in Interviews
and Appraisals

Leverage Your
Connections

PRINCIPLE 1
PRINCIPLE 2
PRINCIPLE 3
PRINCIPLE 4
PRINCIPLE 5
PRINCIPLE 6
PRINCIPLE 7
PRINCIPLE 8

IT'S _ALWAYS_
YOUR MOVE
Purposeful Progress for
Corporate Career Women

kay white

The 8 Proven
Principles of Your
Career Success
Cycle™

"Put blinders on to those things which conspire to hold you back, especially the ones in your own head."

— MERYL STREEP

PRINCIPLE 1:

EMBRACE YOUR EXPANSION TREE

I was anxious, fretting and stuck. Really stuck. The kind of stuck that has you procrastinating and doing everything else but what you know you should be doing. Having just committed to hosting a three-day live event for career women to gather and learn about being the driver of their own career bus, I was stuck.

The chatter inside my head went "Who am I to be able to do this?" "What will everyone think as I step out on stage in this *huge* ballroom in London?" "Who am I to guide, teach, share and lead a hundred women towards career success?" "What if no one comes?" and so on.

Having made an investment in myself and with many mentors and coaches to help guide me on my own path,

I took this sense of doubt to my own mentor, Andrea. I asked her "How do I believe in myself so I can be who I need to be in order to inspire the women who come?"

She told me something that quickly shifted my thinking and gave me the helpful prod I needed to get unstuck along the lines of "Kay, it's kind of like you're a tree. A big, solid, established tree. And for the tree to continue to stay upright through all that life throws at it, for it to expand and grow, the roots must be deep, embedded and stable." That simple metaphor hit home.

There I was with over 20 years of rock-solid corporate experience and leadership. I'd navigated all the highs and lows, mentors and bullies, opportunities and setbacks that had come my way. I'd then gone on to build my own business showing career women clients exactly how to get promoted, valued and rewarded without selling their souls. And I had done all this and more, based on offering what I knew, understood and was open enough to learn.

I realised that I was already the tree Andrea spoke about – the vibrancy and strength that show in the leaves and branches rely on the depth and extent of its roots. Of course I could host my 'Show Up, Sparkle & Be Heard' event. I just had to stop the spinning thoughts in my head and *believe* I could. I needed to stop the chatter of the 'small me' and listen more closely to the 'big me'.

This insight inspired me to create something which now helps career women find themselves, stop the swirling and start believing in and working on working out their own brilliance too. The Expansion Tree came to me when I was at the beautician's, staring into space having my toenails painted. I knew what it should look like and what made up the tree. I understood what was above the surface – what other people see. And I knew what was below – the roots, which enable the tree to grow and stay upright.

I sketched it in my little 'ever-with-me' notepad and then had my designer Erin turn it into something which I now use all the time for my clients and myself. At the event that I had been so worried about, I stood in that massive sparkly ballroom and used the Expansion Tree to start us off on day one. And now you can use it too.

Here's the version I now use in all my workshops. Do study it because we're going to talk about it throughout this book; it is a tool you can continue to use as you expand in your career. Let's start using it right now.

HOW TO USE THE EXPANSION TREE

You'll see that each branch and root has a space for you to rate yourself. There are items that appear above the ground and others that appear below the ground. Rate, on a scale of 1 to 10, how you handle these things at the moment. 1 being low "Oh Kay, I'm hopeless at that" and 10 being high "Yes Kay, I'm comfortable and already on it with that."

Let's start with rating your 'above the surface' factors – the branches – but first, please read the next sections to better understand the terms that I am using and then pick your numbers. This gives you a sense of where to focus most and then see how the dial moves for you as you progress through the book.

To download and print off your own version and use it to rate where you are as you read on, please go to: **www.kaywhite.com/bookresources** where the resources mentioned in the book to support you are waiting for you.

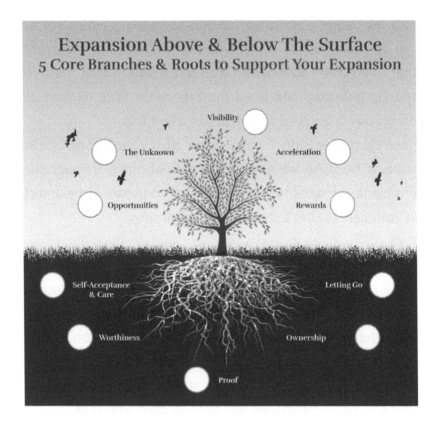

THE BRANCHES
OPPORTUNITIES AND THE UNKNOWN

*'If you're offered a seat on a rocket ship,
don't ask what seat. Just get on.'*

~ SHERYL SANDBERG

The phone rings, you pick it up and you're asked "Hey, will you speak at XYZ Conference next month?" or "Glad I've seen you. We're starting up a new committee; will you be on it representing your sector?" or "I've just been asked about you and I recommended you for a new position at ABC Co."

All these and a myriad more are day-to-day opportunities that come your way. You may not notice them or be so closed off to them that you think they don't exist, but they do. Your ability to say "Yes" to having that first coffee or meeting or saying "OK, tell me a little more" will start to separate you in the Success Cycle. Not having to know all the details, not having to have it all mapped out with a bow on, allowing yourself to be open to what *might* work rather than what won't is where I want you to rate yourself.

The unknown is, by its very name, uncharted water. It's a place where you have to trust yourself enough to say the first – not necessary every – but the first "Yes". So, ask yourself, how comfortable are you with saying "Yes" *before* you have it all worked out and understood? You never do, by the way. Even if you think you do.

HOLLY'S STORY

Holly was a successful lawyer in a city law firm, although she was frustrated with her rate of progress. She'd been mentored by Donald, her boss and colleague of many years, and it didn't really suit Donald to let Holly loose on the partnership trail. She was very much a subordinate but had a brilliant brain, a keen eye for detail and a great rapport with clients. She was ambitious, yet couldn't see her development and partnership track coming to fruition any time soon.

As many women do, Holly believed that if she worked hard enough for long enough, eventually she'd be promoted. What happens though, more often than not, is that you work even harder; making others look good or feel supported with the result that your career goals don't really suit those close to you. They have to let you go and find someone else to do their legwork. I'm not being mean here or unnecessarily cynical but it's human nature to want to work with people you know, like and trust. Why would your boss want to change that? If you want to drive your own career bus and expand, you need to change things up.

When Holly was asked if she'd go along for a meeting by a competitor, her immediate thought was "No thanks, I'm happy where I am and I feel very loyal to the company who've been good to me." Together in a group of career women I mentor called The Sparkle Zone, we encouraged Holly to go along. To say the first "Yes". "What harm can a quick coffee do? Go along and see what they want; what's to lose?"

That was the advice she received from women just like her. Women who knew they also needed to drink their own medicine at times. Maybe this is you too? You'd say the same to Holly I expect, but would you say the same to yourself?

The coffee turned into a very affable but focussed conversation about an opportunity. She'd been noticed by the competition and they were interested in offering her a role. Subsequently, that quick coffee turned into a series of interviews, a job offer, a pay rise and promotion.

JENNIFER'S STORY

My English friend Jennifer was living in Austria raising her family there. Her German had got to a level where she was able to teach Austrian children to speak English. She wasn't always 100 per cent accurate but she could always be understood and, with the benefit of the time to crosscheck, her written German was great.

One day a contact called her and asked if she'd be prepared to take on a piece of paid work to translate an industrial manual. There was a fairly tight timeframe to meet, but it was well paid and something she could do. Here's, though, where we learn about opportunities: they are fleeting.

The person wanted to know that same day if Jennifer would take on the project. She said "Let me think about it and I'll get back to you tomorrow". Asking others, including her husband, and questioning her level of German, she wasn't able to say the first "Yes" there and then. The next day she received an email to say they'd found someone else.

So, here's the thing. She only had to say "Yes, tell me more" or "Yes, send me something over to look at" and she'd have stayed in the game. They most likely wouldn't have gone elsewhere. That's the thing about this particular branch – you need enough to get going but you don't need to know it all. Not straightaway.

JUST A REMINDER ABOUT OPPORTUNITIES

It's important to know what's going on around you and what opportunities there are to stretch yourself. You don't have to know it all before you start or follow a conversation as to where an opportunity may lie. You can buy time. It's likely to be a series of conversations.

Like Holly and Jennifer, you can always say "No thanks" and deselect yourself down the line. The key, though, is to start by saying the first "Yes" to an opportunity you don't fully know about, but have an inkling that you're interested in. It puts you out there; it keeps you in the game. It takes you off the stands and on to the court where the game is being played.

VISIBILITY: IT'S NOT WHO YOU KNOW, IT'S WHO KNOWS YOU

'The power of visibility can never be underestimated.'

~ Margaret Cho

I've lost count of the times I've heard clients say "Oh Kay, I don't really know how I could talk to X; they don't know who

I am" when we're considering how to make a move towards something they want – a promotion, more profile, or the lead role on a project.

Here's the thing about visibility: it's about being seen and known. It's less about being a show-off and a showgirl, which, quite rightly, most people want to avoid. It's more about being on the radar.

So, ask yourself: How comfortable are you being out there?

Out there, by the way, can take on many forms. Speaking up at a meeting instead of shrinking back. Putting yourself in the frame for a presentation or slot on a panel. Offering to update the team or the executive board on a project you've worked on.

It's about being noticed, being seen to add value and being remembered. My question to you is "Who's talking about you when you're not in the room and what are they saying?" If you've been on the radar for the right reasons, then you're going to be more easily remembered and put forward for opportunities as a result.

JANE'S STORY

Working closely with me, my clients are used to being dared. So, I dared Jane, a senior project manager, to do something she wouldn't normally do. Jane wanted to raise her visibility and profile in her industry to be able to see what other roles might be out there. She had a boss who wasn't keen on promoting her because she was doing too good a job at administration for the team. She was bored and frustrated, and knew it was time to do something to make her move either internally or outside the firm.

When she told me that she wanted to go to a networking meeting the following night but hated such events, I dared Jane to go by giving her a 'mission'.

You know the word 'networking' fills most people with dread. Images come up of standing around balancing a glass of something, desperately looking for someone to talk to or working out how to get away from someone who's chewing your ear off telling you how brilliant they are. We've all been there, haven't we?

So, I dared Jane to consider what she wanted to come away with – to set her intention about what it was going to be like. She said she wanted to have good chats, drink only soft drinks, connect with a few people she knew would be there and also see if she could put herself forward to be part of a specialist group who worked across the industry. So far, very specific.

My mission for Jane was to come away with at least three business cards of people she'd be interested to stay in touch with and who she felt she could help or could support her in some way.

That night, when she easily could have been on her sofa at home, Jane met a man called James. His business card was one of the three she collected. Over the following months, James connected her with someone who he knew would want to meet her. From this connection, she was invited to be on a committee, which gave her profile and access to many others in her industry she'd never have otherwise met. One of them approached her regarding a new role and asked if she could put Jane forward, having seen her in action on the committee and having got to know her a little.

It didn't all happen the same day, but Jane was offered a role and negotiated a 50 per cent salary uplift based on her new-found confidence. She asked for what she wanted, demonstrated her value and was prepared to dig into negotiate the salary she knew she deserved. James started this particular ball rolling for her and it came from her being out there, more visible and available to connect.

ACCELERATION: THE NEED FOR SPEED

'The question isn't who's going to let me;
it's who's going to stop me.'

~ AYN RAND

I'm a great advocate of buying yourself more time when you're operating day-to-day at work in conflicting situations or negotiations, or when you're being pushed by someone else and not feeling ready. Buying more time is a strategy (more on that later) but at this point remember that acceleration and the need for speed are the keys.

Ask yourself how long you take to act on instinct or opportunity. Like saying "Yes" before you're ready, the acceleration branch of the tree is about taking inspired action in the moment. Picking up the phone instead of hesitating.

Pressing send on the application rather than checking and chatting with friends. Operating from a place of instinct.

I recommend looking up Mel Robbins' 'The 5 Second Rule' and watching her TED talk to get a fuller flavour. Her theory is that as humans we're hard-wired to avoid or shy away from making decisions. We need encouragement and often affirmation that we're doing the right thing. She advocates 'The 5 Second Rule' to keep you moving on your decisions and stop second-guessing yourself.

Count 5, 4, 3, 2, 1 and take action. The countdown is key. There's nowhere else to go when you count downwards. If you go from 1 to 5, you can cheat and keep going. Who knows where you'll end up?

Imagine that you use this technique when you walk up to the person you want to speak with, apply for that role you've just seen advertised or call that person you've been meaning to ask for a coffee. You get the idea. You accelerate and take action outside of how you normally would.

Expanding into the person you know you want to become means you need to accelerate towards things more than you think you can. You set in motion the next natural move or phase in your development when you get more comfortable with going faster. Not reckless fast. Just faster. Go for something this year, rather than next. Go for something *now* rather than when you've got yet another year's experience, another qualification (a procrastination tactic), or when your boss *tells* you you're ready.

Try going for it now.

You are ready if you have the sense you are. You just are. It can make your head spin a little as you start behaving more this way, but I promise you that what it does do is keep you in the game. It shows you and it shows others that you are capable of instinctive, guided action.

If you look at any successful colleague, friend or entrepreneur, you'll find they accelerate and go for things long before others would or when 'good sense' kicks in. It separates them from the wannabes.

MY STORY

When I first started my online business in 2010, the mentoring group I was part of dared me to write my first book. I was even introduced to Bob, my publisher, who'd written a book about *why* you must write a book.

Instead of my normal listen, think, think, chat, ask, think and wait way of operating, I decided to start writing *The A to Z of Being Understood* on a flight back from San Diego. That was October and, by the following June, I was on stage at a conference in the States with my finished book in my hand. I was talking about the ride of taking action and accelerating far faster than I would ever have before. Sharing this with you isn't to impress you in any way; it's to encourage you to accelerate and trust that whatever happens, you'll handle it.

While writing my book I was encouraged by Lisa, my mentor at that time, to start teaching the principles in the book at the same time as writing it. Again, instead of saying "Oh, I couldn't possibly do that; I'm too busy writing it," I decided to do that too. I offered a six-week teleclass and had seven women register. I had to learn how host a group, plan a call, use technology, process enrolments *and* be the leader. It made me learn and get going because I'd committed to these women that we were doing this together.

There were times when I was only two weeks ahead of my group. My writing would be on 'Q for Questions' in my A to Z book, and the group would be on a call learning about 'L for Listening', 'M for Meaning', 'N for No' and 'O for Open'. I hadn't written beyond Q so I knew I had to keep accelerating towards Z because it felt as if a train was chasing me with my mentoring clients on board.

Do you think I learned a thing or two? Oh my goodness, did I? The book was richer as a result of the feedback I received from these paying clients. My confidence soared as I heard how much the group was learning and what was working for them. I suddenly felt myself surer and more grounded as to why my book was so important.

Within a few months of being published, the book was being taught in a business school in Austria. The tutor asked me whether she could introduce me to the business students who were coming to London as part of their curriculum. Speaking to the group at the Austrian Embassy in London was such a thrill. I said "Yes" long before I had a clue what I'd say or if I could actually stand on my feet and speak about the book. It was a whole other level of learning to do that too.

Again, this isn't about trying to impress you; it's truly about showing you what happens when you go faster than you think you can. You make things happen, learn on the move and attract people and supporters to your cause. That's where you find more opportunities to grow, learn, expand, contribute and be rewarded. You make yourself learn and fill in the gaps as you come up to them. You're in motion and no longer waiting.

REWARDS: YOUR LEVEL OF RECEIVING

'Ask for what you want and be prepared to get it.'

~ MAYA ANGELOU

This branch of your Expansion Tree is about money, recognition and allowing yourself to be rewarded for your contribution. I've lost track of the clients who've told me how fiercely and successfully they negotiate for their team members when it comes to salary reviews or bonus discussions. Here's the irony. They hate doing it for themselves. They block or avoid discussions about money, value and their worth.

Rewards are a vital part of expansion. How can you expect to step up and be promoted or appointed as a senior career woman if you shy away from discussions about your own rewards? The very word 'reward' means recognition for one's service or contribution. It's not only you looking back on the year just gone; it's also about your ability to discuss the plans and responsibilities you have on the horizon and how you're going to rise to meet them and be rewarded for doing so.

Why should anyone else be more interested in your salary, how much holiday you have or your bonus level than you? They're not. They're always more interested in their own and, as we both know, are always looking to save money or shave money from one person's salary to keep a little in reserve for another.

Here are some important questions to ask yourself:

- How comfortable are you negotiating on your own behalf?

- Where are you on your comfort level of taking a discussion about your salary and rewards to your boss?

- Do you plan and prepare for a discussion where you can demonstrate what you've been doing and have a number in mind?

- Do you wait to find out what's on the table when it comes to personal review time or are you dropping little seeds with your boss, or his or her boss, about your contribution?

- Do you only think of money as a reward?

- Are you considering flexible working, interim bonuses, extra holiday and staggered payments?

Most women don't have positive answers to these questions. I know that it's the fastest way to being rewarded and paid what you're worth when you – and only you – are prepared to talk about and ask for what you want. I'm going to show you how to increase your level of receiving and comfort around talking about your value and contribution as we move through *The 8 Principles of Your Career Success Cycle*™ together. Skip to **Principle 6: Negotiate More For Yourself** if this is urgent for you.

ALISON'S STORY

Alison kept hearing from her boss that there was no room to pay her any more despite negotiating and regularly talking about how she felt. Realising she was getting herself stuck and frustrated, she started looking outside her organisation at roles with a salary level she wanted.

Alison and I discussed interview preparation and showing yourself in the best possible light. Through our conversation, she realised was that she didn't want to leave her current company at all. What she knew she needed to do was focus and improve her influencing skills in relation to negotiating her salary. We focussed on strategies and techniques to prepare her for her salary meeting. What Alison shared about this meeting is exactly what I want for you.

Instead of using most of the time to speak about each of her team members, and then squeezing in a last-minute reference to her salary and rewards, she did it differently. Alison started with herself. She focussed on her own developments, the full scope of the role now she understood it more fully and what she had already implemented. She also laid out her plans for the coming year. In that moment, she was even more certain that she deserved consideration for a raise.

It led to a very successful meeting for Alison that paved the way for both a salary increase and a new, bigger opportunity within the organisation. Clearly, Alison prepared for this meeting but most importantly, she had the confidence to put herself *first* for a change.

JUST A REMINDER ABOUT REWARDS

It's always good to remember that most of the time the conversation you have along these lines has to be taken somewhere else to someone else. Giving your boss, manager or lead officer enough time and a strong case to discuss why it's warranted and important is the key. It's also invariably the first of a few conversations, which can free you from the pressure of getting a "yes" in that first meeting.

THE ROOTS

*'My feet are definitely more grounded than before.
And I know that I'm not holding onto a dream.
I'm holding onto my life.'*

~ *CELINE DION*

Having rated yourself on the branches, now it's time to focus on your roots. The roots, which are not seen by anyone else, are felt at your core. The roots hold you steady as the inevitable storms swirl around you at work.

SELF-ACCEPTANCE AND CARE: PUT YOURSELF FIRST FOR A CHANGE

'Nourishing yourself in a way that helps you blossom in the direction you want to go is attainable, and you are worth the effort.'

~ DEBORAH DAY

Women, in general, are at the back of the queue when it comes to looking after ourselves. We tend to put others' needs and wants first, ensuring as far as we can that others are cared for and happy. Then, if there's a shred of energy or attention left, we look at what it is we want and need.

This is a false economy of course. It leads to exhaustion, unhappiness and frustration. To allow yourself to be important enough to go for what you need – exercise, nutrition, sufficient sleep, family time, time off, more interesting projects, promotion opportunities and more – only becomes important and on the radar when *you* choose to make those things important.

Allow yourself to let go of being a version of some superhuman woman who doesn't want to cause a fuss or avoids showing others what she needs. It's self-defeating and dangerous. Instead, be prepared to look at what you need and want to be effective and discuss it directly rather than hint or moan about it to others.

Be more "self-ish" not selfish. Care a little less about everyone else and a little more about yourself. When you're on a plane and the crew runs through the safety procedures, one of the instructions is to "put your oxygen mask on first". How can you help those around you if you're starving of oxygen yourself? The irony is often that by forgetting to look after ourselves, we end up needing to be looked after by others.

So, this root is grounded in you being clearer about what it is you need to feel good, be healthy and allowing your own precious life-force energy to be as important – no, more important – than others'.

WORTHINESS: YOUR SENSE OF BEING ENOUGH

'You are enough.'

~ THE UNIVERSE

Worthy is one of those words that can set your teeth jangling. Am I worthy of this? Who am I to be worthy or deserving? It's a self-reflection and a decision that you make for you and about you. Being enough. Smart enough. Experienced enough. Clever enough. Fun enough. Kind enough. Worthy enough and so it goes.

As a root for your Expansion Tree, worthiness is a tricky one to measure because it's often a sense you have. If you say to yourself "I don't deserve this" or "people will think I'm too big for my boots if…" then this is where your worthiness muscle needs exercising and strengthening.

This branch has a touch of the Rewards branch – your ability to receive which is a more visible thing. The Worthiness root is how comfortable and how deserving you feel for what you attract and make happen in your life. Understanding your own sense of worthiness and deserving is being able to ask yourself "Who, if not me?" and "If not me, why someone else?"

You'll often find there isn't anyone else you know who should be doing, contributing or handling what you are. It's just you need to get used to the feeling – the sense of you being enough to handle it. So now let's see how you rate yourself around your role and your sense of what's next for you.

ELLIE L'S STORY

Ellie encountered this question and crossroads about worthiness for the first time in a long time when she realised an ambition. She had recently been appointed as a board director of a National Health Trust and it struck her, as she prepared for her first full board meeting "Who am I to be at this board table?"

It's easy to doubt yourself when you're on the precipice of doing something you've not done before. In Ellie's case, it was something she had done before – participating in high-level meetings, offering input and advice on the financials and being prepared to take a stand on something. These were all already part of her skill set. So where did the doubt or the question of worthiness come from?

Together, we looked at Ellie's path, her career history and all the experience she had from the various places she'd worked. We discussed some of her key life lessons, background and family values as we prepared her for this meeting. It's easy to forget all that you've done, achieved, experienced and handled in these moments of questioning "Just who do you think you are to be doing this?" and to forget exactly *who* you are to be doing it.

It's not to say there haven't been moments where Ellie felt out of her depth but instead of them being permanent, they're moments. They're fleeting and if, like her, you can remind yourself of all you do know and have done rather than focussing on the gaps, then you can trust yourself too. As I asked Ellie "Well, if not you Ellie, who should be there instead?" True to form, she couldn't think of anyone else who should be there instead of her because they'd appointed her based on her skills and experience, and she had tons of both. She'd allowed herself to momentarily forget.

PROOF:
FIND AND KEEP EVIDENCE OF
YOUR SUCCESS AND SKILLS

'You are braver than you believe, stronger than you seem and smarter than you think.'

~ A. A. MILNE IN 'WINNIE THE POOH'

Do you know how it is when someone asks you to talk about recent successes and you stare back at them blankly? Or when you're coming up to your crucial personal review time and you're scrambling to remember what's happened over the year? Or what about when – yikes – you finally decide it's time to update or actually create your CV or resumé? Do you stare at your screen wondering what you've been involved in or made happen in your current role and previous roles?

A game-changing switch you can make is to track proof of your experience, skills, successes and lessons when you're looking at your career in the long-term and not just for the job you have now. Proof gives you an invisible cloak of confidence. That means keeping a log of what you're doing and how you are making things happen. It is immediately reassuring and inspiring to be able to tap into the evidence quickly.

Too often we are being Betty Boo and busy 'doing-the-do'. We forget to track our progress, the developments and the feedback we receive. As a business owner myself, one of the most reassuring things I can do when I'm either feeling stuck or questioning what I'm planning is to go to my Success Swipe File. This is a place where I put feedback I've received, notes from clients, Facebook posts and other success stories. It contains hundreds of stories, things I've created, tried, taught, shared, started, stopped and learned from.

This book is being written based on just some of what's in my own Success Swipe File. How else could I share with you how these ideas and inspirations work if I hadn't tested them and had the feedback of women just like you to reassure us both that it all works?

So, my suggestion is to create your version of a Success Swipe File and track dates you started things, developments, who said what, email blurbs when someone thanks you or gives you feedback about what's happened; and where you've got evidence of income generated or saved, percentages of growth, savings, market share and the like.

It doesn't have to be a perfect science, but it does need to be continually updated. What this does is free you to know that when the day comes, you can draw upon evidence – hard proof if you will – that will enable you to discuss developments, rewards and opportunities from a place of confidence and certainty. You won't need loads of notice because you will be able to quote what people said and clients' successes as a result of your work together with industry developments that your work feeds into. All these and more will be immediately accessible. More than anything, your roots will be deeper and more solid because you understand the extent of what you do and what it's done.

TRACY'S STORY

The key for Tracy was finding a quick and easy way to keep track of positives –whether that was great feedback from a manager or stakeholder; a piece of work she was proud of; an intranet article about the importance of a project she'd worked on. It all counted.

Tracy found it difficult to find time during the week for reflection and before she knew it, it was appraisal time and she was struggling to remember what she'd done. So, she set up a form of 'swipe' file in which she kept these reminders and prompts to flesh out the story of her developments and contributions when she needed them.

It has become something of a treasure trove and a great starting point when Tracy finds herself looking at a blank page when, for example, trying to work out where to start for her mid-year review. It also makes sure she remembers key experiences, particularly those that might have been ad hoc rather than connected to an ongoing project, as well as challenges that have been overcome.

Tracy recently attended a seminar that made her rethink how often she visits the folder. It's always been good for a quick 'pick me up' if she's been feeling a bit negative, but her recent idea is to try to reflect at the end of each week on what she's done that week that made her feel proud. It's so smart to keep an eye on what you're actually doing, being involved in, noticing, learning, and contributing. But do this in the moment rather than, as is so often done, as a last-minute scramble before an appraisal or review.

OWNERSHIP: OWNING YOUR PART, SKILLS, INPUT AND EXPERIENCE

'Career progression often depends on taking risks and advocating for oneself – traits that girls are discouraged from exhibiting.'

~ SHERYL SANDBERG

Taking ownership and acknowledging your own part in results is crucial to your visibility, confidence and others' confidence in you. Along the lines of receiving rewards and putting yourself forward for financial recognition, taking ownership and staking your claim to results is key to your own expansion.

Women tend to be very generous to everyone else when talking about and demonstrating the results and levels of success in their team. "The team were amazing on the ABC Project and their commitment to get the job done never waivered" or "Bob really stepped up and made it happen." Yet, if someone actually tries to acknowledge a woman as the successful contributor, she often brushes it off or accredits the success to someone or something else – a boss, a colleague, team, market conditions, timing or luck.

Do you do this? If so, it is so unfair on you. It is part of our expansion to allow our own success to shine through. You don't have to be a selfish show-off. Let's be honest, we all know one or two of those who take credit for themselves.

However, we can include our input into the feedback, updates and lessons about work we're involved in without being a show-off. In Principle 3, I'm going to give you structures to be able to say things in a way that is both comfortable and allows your part to shine. For now, just think about how comfortable you are with owning your own success, input and contribution.

I believe a factor which comes into play in owning your own success is the natural tendency women have for collaboration and collaborative relationships. It's primal, and I love that we're like this. However, for the purposes of your own career success, you need to be able to toot your own horn without blowing your own trumpet. If you don't, others will question your ability to operate on your own instincts, produce results and talk about your skills, experience and wisdom.

It can sound like this: "Yes, Project ABC was tough. One of my biggest lessons when we hit a wall on the budgets was to go back to the drawing board. I pulled in a few favours from the finance team to check all our numbers and spending levels and then made the decision to reduce the amount of overtime authorised. It focussed our minds and I'm proud that we brought the project in under budget. One of the biggest lessons I've learned is to constantly check the numbers rather than let the excitement of the project run away with us."

Of course, the paragraph above is fictitious, but you can sense there's a level of me *and* us in there which is comfortable, informative and truthful as far as how you own your part in the success and outcome of something. There's a level of risk, naturally, of putting yourself squarely in the frame. But I believe the risk is far greater by undervaluing or underplaying your part in things. Your sense of yourself and how rooted you feel in your experience comes from acknowledging you actually have the experience. A lot of it, in fact.

ELIZABETH'S STORY

When Elizabeth and I started working together on her frustration at her career stalling, one of her biggest blocks was being able to comfortably talk about her successes and skills. She said it was so difficult for her that she almost choked on the words. Together we looked at her Expansion Tree and worked our way around it like you are currently doing. Elizabeth, like so many women, was great at sharing the success of projects with her team and giving the team and others positive feedback. She just wasn't good at receiving it or advocating for herself. She felt uncomfortable owning the success of her contribution.

Working in the finance and tech side of an international bank, Elizabeth had been involved in many projects from the ground up. Her bread and butter was understanding complex information and processes quickly, explaining them simply to a variety of different stakeholders and then helping them join the dots.

What was happening, however, was that Elizabeth felt as if she was going backwards. The ground had shifted around her. Teams had been restructured and then restructured again. Her reporting line was at best blurry and at worst confused. She'd had five bosses in four years, been in four different teams and was moved between a number of different functional groups, which changed sometimes before the ink was dry. This had damaged both her confidence and her earning capacity because no-one was really sure how effective Elizabeth was, including her.

In times like these, where change is the only reliable force you can guarantee is on the horizon, you must understand and own the contribution you make and how it affects the bigger picture of the organisation you work in. It's not enough to hope your boss or his or her boss notices and knows. Most of the time they're too busy trying to drive their own bus and keep an eye on the fuzzy reporting lines they have. You're expected to have a handle on your own input and contribution. You must restructure yourself.

One of the things that shifted Elizabeth's thinking was when I asked her in what has been described to me as a 'care-frontational' way "If not now Elizabeth, when? When are you going to be able to do this for yourself?" It was as if a light turned on. Instead of backing away or deflecting praise and recognition, Elizabeth decided it was time to truly recognise and own her contribution and to join the dots in complicated projects and processes.

She also worked at understanding the monetary value of her work to the bank. It's not always easy to find this out, but you can normally look at the next steps of your work and what it feeds into, and make a conservative estimate. It's surprising and, more often than not, will take your breath away.

Once this became a natural state for Elizabeth and she practiced owning what she was doing, making happen, building and saving, she was approached by not one but two partners in the bank who wanted her on their team. She leveraged one opportunity for the other.

The other development was the awareness that she had 'walk-ability'. She didn't need to feel fear about being stuck or overlooked anymore. She was prepared to walk and take all that experience and potential somewhere else. That's a game changer, and we'll look at that together later in the book. For now, consider your own ownership abilities. They really matter.

LETTING GO: ALLOW YOUR GOOD ENOUGH TO BE GREAT

'Want to be happy? Stop trying to be perfect.'

~ Brené Brown

Ironically, one of the qualities that stands most in the way of being worthy and feeling worthy is perfectionism – not being able to let go of the need to be and do things 'perfectly' – whatever that is.

Does this scenario fit you? You almost missed a deadline because you can't quite trust that you've got it right and it is good enough. You can get into a tangle over-preparing and investing too much time in a piece of work before you show or involve anyone. You end up exhausted and full of doubt. You are afraid of being judged less-than-perfect.

Join the crowd. I have heard from hundreds of clients who repeatedly second-guess that of themselves about whether something is good enough, perfect, or even worse, absolutely perfect.

Here's the catch. Everything – and yes, I do mean everything – is subjective. Your idea of perfect will be different from mine. Your perfect meal, holiday, partner, outfit, role or evening will be different from mine and from that of everyone else you know. That's the myth about perfection. It doesn't exist. You can then recognise that when you're in the spin of constantly tweaking, trying too hard or over-thinking the detail, you are in perfection quicksand. It can slow you down and stop you making a move. Perfection. It's only your version of it.

What I've learned in my own journey as a recovering perfectionist and through coaching and mentoring thousands of career women is that when you accept that you are good enough, your version of what's good-to-go frees you up, allows you to keep things moving and invites input from others.

And let's be honest. If you have perfectionist tendencies, then your version of good enough is likely going to be miles more comprehensive and well thought-out than someone who doesn't care that much and could be considered slapdash.

The important distinction here as you look at self-acceptance is that you don't get sucked into the whole 'it's got to be perfect' quicksand because you fear criticism or being judged 'less than' in some way. You're always going to put the time and thought into what you're doing, but you're going to allow yourself to trust yourself. I no longer use the word 'perfect' very often. When someone says to me "Here you go Kay" I say "OK great, thanks" or "Brilliant, thanks" – never "Perfect". It won't be. And that's OK.

To quote the great writer, Margaret Atwood, who wrote *The Handmaid's Tale:* 'If I waited for perfection I'd never write a word.'

ELLIE M'S STORY

Ellie was a private client who used the word 'perfect' all the time. She was ambitious, driven and always looking to get things right. She was frustrated with some of her colleagues who she felt didn't go the extra mile like she did but seemed to be doing well. She couldn't understand it.

It didn't seem fair to her that she would be working into the small hours preparing a presentation or a team update, and her colleagues would come with the headlines of what was happening and seem to wing it. This is just a small example of what Ellie noticed, and she thought it was a reflection on others and not on her.

She found she was exhausted and stressed. Her heart would sink if she was asked to prepare something for tomorrow because she knew she'd be up that night looking at all the angles and preparing every last detail.

When Ellie noticed her skin was looking really pallid and grey, and her lovely long dark hair was starting to come away in clumps, she knew she had to do something. Having strived for perfection, Ellie was making herself sick. Really sick.

She had to make dramatic changes and end the cycle of skipping meals, eating quick fix meals rather than nourishing ones and feeling she was always on the cusp of being found out as being less-than-perfect. Ellie turned her life and her lifestyle around by looking at her way of behaving and the pressure she was putting on herself – no one else was pressurising her in the way she was – and by researching how nutrition affects everything in your body including the stress, which can lead to alopecia and hair loss.

She decided to enrol in a course to qualify as a nutrition and well-being expert. She negotiated working compressed hours so that she could take the time off she needed to study. While this has turned her life around, she acknowledges that she can still strive for that elusive perfection.

Now, however, she goes for her version of good enough. She knows she's diligent, smart, ambitious and caring. She also knows she can stray over to the dark side of that perfection paralysis. She notices now when it feels like she's heading that way and reminds herself of the dark days of illness and hair loss. Now she's able to see and recognise when enough is enough and trusts herself to always be enough. Good enough.

Ellie's story is one of a myriad of client stories I could choose from about recovering perfectionists who allowed themselves to let go enough to trust their version of good enough. I do so hope you'll do the same. You free yourself and ground yourself with this root of self-acceptance and care by allowing perfection to be the myth it truly is.

BEFORE WE MOVE ON

The essence of the Expansion Tree is that it's always growing and shifting for you. You'll have days, months and years when you'll rate higher in some areas than in others, but that's the point of this book. It's a cycle. It's continuous. When you change roles or organisations, start projects, manage different people or change your own boss, refer to your Expansion Tree and remind yourself where you are and what you want to focus on now.

So, let's move into looking more widely and carefully at opportunities by discussing **Principle 2: Discover What's Out There.** Again, remember – keep one eye on where you are now and one eye on where you want to be going.

"Noticing small changes early helps you adapt to the bigger changes that are to come."

– Dr Spencer Johnson
(Who Moved My Cheese?)

PRINCIPLE 2:

DISCOVER WHAT'S OUT THERE

It can feel overwhelming when you sense it's time to move on. Or you can decide to consider it exciting, full of opportunity and new openings. We do get to choose how we experience the world through our mental state. Looking at things as opportunities rather than problems changes our state and, in turn, our actions.

In my book, *The A to Z of Being Understood*, the letter A was for Attitude, The Angle Your Nose Meets The Wind. If you see your quest for a new, elevated or more fulfilling role as an opportunity for growth, then it's going to be you changing your attitude.

After you do the research and look at what's out there, you may decide you're happier where you are. But that's by making enquiries and some calculated moves, not by just settling. This is what this Principle is all about – making calculated and considered moves, taking in feedback and angling your nose to meet the winds of change.

INDUSTRIES & DEVELOPMENTS: WHAT'S GOING ON?

'Begin doing what you want to do now. We are not living in eternity. We only have this moment, sparkling like a star in our hand and melting like a snowflake…'

~ FRANCIS BACON

Have you ever said out loud or to yourself "But it's all I've ever done" or "But it's all I know" when you consider either moving outside of or to a different role in your industry?

What do I mean by industry? As an ex-insurance broker, my industry was insurance, which is part of the overarching financial services industry. My part in it was sales or broking. I sold contracts relating to risk. The skills I acquired selling legally binding, multi-million dollar contracts could have set me on a completely different career selling products, real estate, holidays or even widgets. Why? Because I developed skills of negotiating, finding the sweet spot for a deal, building relationships and translating information from technical to everyday language through working hard, modelling others and riding many highs and lows. The industry was just where I was using those skills at the time.

Your industry might be within the energy, charity, healthcare, legal, banking, retail, entertainment or education sectors, or something else. You get the essence that the industry is the overarching space where your organisation operates and you currently fit. What you actually *do* within your industry may be specialised. What people forget is that skills can be applied and brought to other industries more easily than assumed. So often there's a belief that if you have all your experience in one industry, then it will be virtually impossible to come out of it into another. That's another myth.

Looking at industries and the developments within them is part of *The 8 Principles of Your Career Success Cycle*™. It gives you the sense – which won't always suit your boss or your organisation – that you already have a unique set of skills which, when packaged and expressed to suit another industry, are eminently transferrable. If indeed, you want them to be.

Understanding where your industry is in its own cycle of success is something few people look at closely. Be prepared to regularly ask yourself searching questions about how the land lies and what you see on the horizon so that you are ready to embrace inevitable change.

Ask yourself a few deep-dive questions about where you are now:

o How is the industry developing?

o Who are the current big players?

o What are the foreseeable threats?

- Where could there be opportunities based on what's happening?

- What is it I love about the industry?

- What do I find tough about it?

- What is our industry's main purpose and how well are we doing?

- Who seems to be making the most money in our industry?

- Who are the unsung heroes?

- What do I see happening in five years in our industry?

- Where do I want to fit into that and do I really want to?

- What would I tell someone like me to do if they asked my advice?

Here's what I want you to really embrace: *Change is happening all the time in every industry and each change in one industry affects change in another.*

Think of all the effects outside of the tobacco industry when bans were enforced on advertising smoking. Consumption was threatened, advertisers had to look at new ways to reach and try to reassure consumers, health organisations jumped on being able to support people stopping smoking and industries sprang up to find ways for people to get nicotine without a cigarette. Recently, a whole new industry with a whole different set of risks and opportunities has come from the vaping industry. Change always ripples outwards and affects a myriad of other industries, which is where threats and opportunities are continually found.

For the purposes of your own career, I invite you to keep a watchful eye on your industry. Don't become complacent with where you are or think you're stuck there. Neither serves you well or makes you feel real confidence in the long term.

Knowing – not hoping – is what will give you confidence. If you understand your skills, you will be able to move within your industry as it moves or to move outside of it and join another one. Everything is cyclical. As women, we are attuned to our own cycles so let's stay more aware of industry cycles too.

Every year for five years, I sent out a little book to everyone registered for a three-day live event I hosted for ambitious career women. The book was called *Who Moved My Cheese?* by Dr Spencer Johnson. This simple, quick-to-read parable is a message for the reader to stay alert, avoid complacency and notice when the cheese – cheese being a metaphor for what you value – is changing or disappearing. This book encourages the reader to 'smell the cheese often so you know when it's getting old' rather than to pretend change is not happening. Arriving at the event, women had already had their senses piqued towards noticing and embracing change rather than ignoring or fearing it.

Rather than being caught out by the change – or your cheese moving without you noticing – keep yourself plugged into what is happening. Notice what's being said in the press. Read trade journals at least once a month. Find someone who you trust within the industry to translate a little of what they see happening. Go to conferences or events you might normally avoid. Information is power and sensing what's on the horizon in a more conscious way is a big part of keeping you nimble, current and prepared to move with the cheese.

Here are a few signs or red flags for you to notice. They may give you the sense that your own cheese is moving or, in truth, has already moved.

Red Flags!

○ The work you used to find challenging and stretching feels as if you're going through the motions and up to a point you can cruise through your day

○ The people you used to enjoy working with have either now left or have had their own change of circumstances – it doesn't feel as much fun somehow

○ Your boss has moved and restructures keep happening, which means you're feeling adrift without someone who really knows how much you contribute

○ You've had big shifts at home – maybe got married, maybe split up with your partner, maybe had a child or maybe trying for a child or maybe moved home and now have a much longer commute – and priorities have changed

o You've been passed over for a promotion opportunity again and this time it's too hard to see someone less experienced than you doing what you believe you were ready for and being paid what you know you should be being paid

o You can't imagine being in the same position in 12 months' time: it makes you mad and sad to imagine it

o You feel like you're a wallflower hiding in the shade and it doesn't seem to make any difference what you do; you're not being taken seriously like you used to be

o Sunday nights have a feeling of doom or a sense of 'here we go again', which is you spinning your wheels

o Your industry is consolidating with major technology or compliance changes

o Your organisation is involved in a takeover or merger and where does that leave you?

o You know this is your one precious life and that work is just part of it, not all of it, and you know if someone were to ask your advice if they felt like you do, you'd say "get a grip woman and do something about it." You know you would and so do I; it's so easy when it's not you though.

One of the best things you can do for yourself is to take control, drive the bus and guide your own life, rather than wait for someone to tell you what you 'should' do. No one is more interested in your career progress or aspirations than you so take back the steering wheel, look more closely at the road ahead and drive.

SONAL'S STORY

Sonal could sense it was time to do something different. For a while she'd been watching the oil and energy industry shake with the price of oil fluctuating wildly, projects being shelved, people being made redundant, and more uncertainty creeping into her project management area of expertise.

As a client who has been inside my group mentoring circle, The Sparkle Zone, for a while, Sonal wanted to make herself heard and was keen to find a new role with more challenges in a different industry. Instead of thinking "Well, I only know the oil industry," she wanted to target the investment banking industry instead.

For a while, Sonal had watched what was happening in the banking industry with the massive and sweeping changes which were designed to make the sector more robust, compliant and sustainable. She saw the potential to use her project management skills in a different capacity.

After more than three interviews, Sonal was offered a role in the investment banking side of one of the big global banks based in Canary Wharf, London. It was a testament to the power of intention and focus. Using input and guidance from friends and colleagues, doing plenty of her own research, learning the language and issues of the industry and being prepared to talk about her plans to cross from one industry to another, she got a role and proved that you *can* use your experience and know-how to translate them to another industry.

Of course, you have to do the work of making it clear and relevant to those you want to listen. If you can make your case with passion and conviction, which Sonal did, you can move with the cheese.

Two further noteworthy points from Sonal's story. First, she was concerned she'd flunked her final interview. She was a little later in arriving than she would have liked. In order to settle herself and, feeling a bit flustered, she was looking at her emails on her telephone when they called her in. She noticed the difference in her concentration and anxiety levels. Fortunately, she'd done well enough already, but it's noteworthy that you have to stay focussed and ignore outside stimulation when you want to show up at your best. It takes presence and being present. We'll talk more about that when we get to **Principle 5: Shine in Interviews and Appraisals.**

Second, it has not been plain sailing for Sonal since arriving in the investment banking world. A series of changes and shifts in management structure meant she was working for someone who had not interviewed her and had no idea who she was since the person who had hired her was redeployed. These things can't be planned, but what can be is to stay connected to your skills and to know that if – as it may have for Sonal – your cheese has moved again, so you must be prepared to do the same. Getting stuck sometimes happens. *Staying* stuck is a choice.

AGENCIES AND HOW TO HANDLE THEM'

*Taking chances on opportunities, even if they
aren't right for you, gives you a clearer picture
of where you want to go with your life and your career.'*

~ LAUREN BUSH

Companies often prefer to only use the services of recruiters as they weed candidates out. A recruitment agency has a pool of potential candidates and connections to draw upon and typically will arrange the preliminary interviews and ensure CVs match the post's criteria. It's a service and normally the agent receives a healthy percentage of the candidate's first year's salary from the organisation for providing the gateway to the right candidate.

Remembering this when you decide to approach or respond to an agency for your new move is key to establishing yourself in the relationship. You are part commodity and part client. It's easy to forget and assume the agency has all the power. They do and they don't. Agencies fulfil a service. They need someone like you to be paid at all. It's easy to forget this and believe that you're just a number when, in fact, you do need each other.

I always recommend that clients ask the agent they're speaking to about their service levels and actually say that you're looking to work with an agency you can trust. Ask probing questions about their fulfilment ratio. How long do they typically take to fill a role? What is their follow-up service? Why do their clients use them? Shift the energy to one of partnership rather than you being the one in need.

If you've been approached, then you can ask questions like "How do you stay in touch with your candidates?" and "I'm assuming you don't leave your candidates hanging about decisions?" and other questions that show you're not to be messed with. It doesn't unfortunately mean you won't be, but this approach shows that you're not just passive and super-grateful. There are many agencies, and they're all in competition with each other for placing the successful candidate who, of course, may well be you.

If you're doing the initial approaching and registering yourself with an agency, do ensure you say why you've chosen them. It may be because you see the extent of interesting roles they seem to be offering. It may be because you were recommended, in which case, say by whom and why.

It's about you establishing a relationship as quickly as you can and saying you've chosen them. 'Chosen' is a subtle word. Never underestimate the power of telling someone you've chosen him or her. It implies you've done research and made a selection based on certain criteria. We *all* like to be chosen.

It's also an easy-breezy thing to say "I've registered with three key agencies, including yourselves, as I'm committed to moving this year and want to be represented by the most professional and successful ones." Clearly, you put your own goal in here such as finding a promotion, different industry, or accelerated progression.

Make sure you don't overdo things if you're unhappy where you are. You don't want to bleat about how mean your boss is or how fed up you are with waiting for things to happen. Be as objective as you can be about how things are where you are now. As you know, you could be perceived as a moaner or someone who let's things get her down. That's not the impression you want to give at all.

Let's say you *are* really fed up where you are and feel stuck and undervalued. It's taken you a while to get fed up enough to do something about it. You know you're heading for some kind of fork in the road. Here's how it could sound if you were to be objective and proactive, rather than fed up and reactive:

"So, I've decided it's time to move on from ABC Company after five years because I'm ambitious and ready to take on more responsibility. There have been a number of restructures where I am which have left a lot of people feeling out of their depth and I don't see the opportunity for me to step up. After five years with regular pay increases and positive appraisals but no advancement opportunity, despite putting myself forward, I know I'm ready to contribute at a higher level and open to what's out there. I'm actively looking for a role where I can use my skills and experience, and also where I can learn and develop."

THE CAR MODEL

A great way to sound objective and proactive is to use the CAR model as mentioned in the book *Lead With A Story* by Paul Smith. Penny, one of my clients and a co-host on some of my mentoring calls and events, described this model at an event we hosted together on Presenting With Presence; she was encouraging our audience to become better storytellers. Stories teach, sell, inspire and influence. We remember them. Often you won't remember the teaching of a principle, but you will remember the story. If the story's well crafted, it's easy to remember since the message is embedded in there.

The CAR model is a simple, easy-to-remember structure into which you can drop a story with the right amount of detail. It allows you to sound objective and proactive. We'll use this model in other places in this book.

> *C is for Context.* What was happening or what is happening relevant to the story? What situation did you, or whoever you're talking about, find themselves in?

> *A is for Action or Actions.* What did you do or what are you doing? What has happened either by your own actions or by what's happened around you

> *R is for Results.* What has evolved? What difference did it make? What's the situation now and the outcome of these actions?

Let's put a few examples of things you might be asked inside the CAR Model.

'So why are you leaving ABC Company?'

Context: There have been a number of restructures which have left a lot of people feeling out of their depth and I don't see the opportunity for me to step up.

Actions: After five years with regular pay increases and positive appraisals but no advancement opportunity, despite putting myself forward, I know I'm ready to contribute at a higher level and open to what's out there.

Results: I'm actively looking for a role where I can use my skills and experience, and also where I can learn and develop".

'Give us an example when you've acted swiftly on your own initiative.'

Context: "We'd just introduced a new type of cover for our clients and we were abroad on a roadshow promoting it and demonstrating how beneficial it would be. Our London office alerted us that there was an error in the presentation, which we'd already shown to a number of clients and had sent directly to a number of others.

Actions: I immediately called my boss and told her that this had happened in case she received any calls. I then called the clients we'd been to see and explained that in our keenness to show them the product there was an error, which we would immediately rectify, and apologised for any confusion.

Results: My boss appreciated the heads-up and my initiative in calling our clients without excuses but with swift honesty and action, and in partnership".

Now you try. Don't overthink this but just keep the structure in mind as you try this out.

'What is it that tells you it's time to drive your own bus in your career?'

Context:

Actions:

Results:

To feel you can always respond without overloading your listener or reader gives you power in these challenging and sometimes on the spot moments.

"Structure gives you freedom" as one of my early mentors Lisa Sasevich used to say. Following a structure enables you to slot the pieces of your story in where they're needed most and keeps you briefer and on point.

MEENA'S STORY

Meena knew it was time to move. She was absolutely sick and tired of feeling sick and tired. Boredom was setting in as well as knowing that there was no chance of promotion in the near future. Her role had changed shape more times than she could remember, and her boss had also been 'restructured' so she wasn't working for the person who attracted her to her role. She was working for someone who was micromanaging her and also taking credit for her input with his boss.

When we met at one of my events, Meena knew it was time for her to do something about how things were. She felt as if she was drifting. Being very ambitious and successful along her career path as well as being happily married with two children, Meena said that now was her time to accelerate and really capitalise on her experience and her passion for AI. Artificial Intelligence for us non-techies.

What Meena taught me was how proactive you can be when working with agencies and how to make it work for you. She'd been approached several times by recruiters before getting to that 'OK, I've had enough' stage where she was actively ready to move.

In the meantime, she'd done something a lot of clients don't do, at least at first. Instead of batting off approaches by headhunters and recruitment agents, she'd actively been interested and open to conversations about what was on offer, what and who they were looking for, and why. She'd taken meetings so she'd have interview practice and had become very comfortable talking about her skills and experience, even though she wasn't remotely interested in the role.

Women have told me they feel disloyal or uncomfortable going to discuss other roles when, in fact, all you're doing is keeping your ears and eyes open to what's out there, what roles are paying, what your experience might be worth elsewhere, and – more often than not – working out that you might be better off where you are. It's kind of like having a measuring stick that helps you understand more about your value, worth and options. So, rather than saying "No, I'm not looking right now" Meena had been saying "OK, tell me a little more about it and why me?"

When Meena was at one of my two-day private client retreats, she mentioned she was going to have a telephone interview with an agent. She was excited about the role, which was working for a niche investment bank that was committed to using cutting edge technology and AI in their process functions. The interview went well. She said she was used to conversations like that and asked as many questions as the interviewer did.

That's the thing for us to remember – that these kinds of situations are conversations. Two-way conversations. Not a grilling of you where you're feeling as if you're going to be caught out or found out, but more of a conversation between professionals. They're also great practice for you.

After a second interview, the recruiter got back in touch to say that Meena wouldn't be put forward for this role because her experience wasn't as in-depth as they were looking for. However, they asked if they could put her forward for another role.

When the time came and the role was a fit, Meena made her move swiftly.

She built in time to have a break between Christmas and New Year and negotiated a start date and lead-in period.

She also decided to beef up her technology experience and qualifications by investing privately in some courses before she started because she knew the gaps in her knowledge.

This all came from engaging in conversations with agents and recruiters and networks. Instead of them being something to avoid, these conversations are actually something to seek out. Not weekly, of course, but without hesitating. See what's out there and use the services of a recruiter. They need you as much, if not more, than you need them.

RESEARCH: CASTING YOUR NET AND FOCUSSING IN

> *'Research is formalised curiosity. It is poking and prying with a purpose.'*

> ~ *ZORA HEALE HURSTON*

It does help, of course, if you know what you're looking for. The more specific you can be about what you want and don't want, the easier it is to hone in on. When you know the part of the business or industry that you want to focus on, the easier it is for others to help you.

For example, if you want to work for ABC Banking Company because you see how well they're doing in the press and know from your colleague that they're recruiting and have a salary scale that is attractive, then I recommend focusing on that company like a laser beam.

Read up about them in the press, cross-reference your network on LinkedIn, focus on them via recruiters and speak to friends and colleagues and let them know you want to find a way in.

When you focus like this based on what you sense or know, you start to do two things quickly. First, you become more of an expert in that company and what they stand for, who's who in the zoo and what their results look like. These days so much information is available on the Internet that there's no excuse to say you don't know anyone. We are all one or two clicks away from information or introductions if we invest time to search or ask for it.

Second, you start to notice things and attract conversations. With the Law of Attraction premise, what you focus on expands. Just as when you decide to buy, for example, a Black Audi TT, you start to notice them more than ever before. Your attention is tuned towards seeing them. The same happens when you focus on a company or an industry.

If you don't have a clue which company or industry you want to direct your attention to, you can still hone in on some of the details, which will support your research.

GET INTO THE DRIVING SEAT WHEN RESEARCHING

Ask friends or contacts of yours about their role and/or industry, but not in a quick-chat-over-a-glass-of-wine way – more in a tell-me-the-down-and-dirty-details kind of way. Ask them searching questions about:

○ How they got to where they have

○ What they love about what they do

- ○ What they don't like

- ○ What plans they have for their career

- ○ What they've done when they've been stuck

- ○ What they see on the horizon in their company

- ○ What challenges their industry are facing, what sort of people seem to be doing well

- ○ And – this key question – what do they see you doing or think you could be good at based on what they know about you? So often others see it before we do.

When you receive responses or input from research like this, don't dismiss anything. Really, don't. As you build up a profile of information and insights, you might have a Eureka! moment or, more likely, someone else will have one for you.

I can't tell you how many times I might say to a client "Well, from what you're telling me, if you were to be told this by someone else, what would you say to them?" This irritating but incisive question often leads to an insight that's easier to see once removed. We all have times when we can clearly see someone doing something or not doing something long before they can. So, ask yourself the question along the lines of "What would I tell someone to do about this?" because it will invariably tell you what you need or want to do too.

Treat the research phase as a project, not as a chore. As I've said before and know to be true, no one is more interested in your career success than you should be. When you take that on and own the responsibility of driving your own career bus forward, you don't let confusion, pushbacks or disappointments stop or slow you down.

Instead, use them as part of the path. Just like Roomba™, our robotic vacuum cleaner: if it comes to a block on its path cleaning around our home, it re-evaluates what's around and doesn't stop or keep pushing over the same spot. It heads off somewhere else around the block.

Sometimes, your next role finds you. You'll have a call from someone, be put forward for something or see a role advertised on your job board at work or online. While the onus is on you to make the move, call back or send in your CV, you still have the opportunity to dig about online. Look at the language of the advertisement or the way the role's been described. Look at who or what is moving and shaking in the industry. Look at the company's competitors and what they're doing or saying about themselves. It all builds up a picture for you that will add to your credibility and confidence when you come to the part about what you can do and what you will bring if they pick you and you pick them.

Researching and profiling something is what we do naturally. When we're thinking of going to a certain location for a holiday, we cross-reference the hotels and the recommendations. We use recognised feedback sites like TripAdvisor™ to find out what others think or have experienced. It's just the same for your career. It's just that it's so much more important.

It amazes me how passive we can be as women. Remember, I know how passive I was and how I let things slide for too long rather than drive my own bus. Rather than putting the magnifying glass up to our eyes and digging about, we wait and assume things will find us. Or we tell ourselves we'll find out more *if* something happens.

The pre-emptive strike approach is what I recommend. Make yourself a swipe-file for that industry or company. Snaffle away links or articles, quotes or stories you find or hear into that file. The day you need them is the day you don't want to be scrambling around trying to remember or find those examples again. You, of course, want to be able to say "Yes, of course, tomorrow works. Let me bring my notes with me as I have questions to ask you too."

As you know, I believe we are always in a career success cycle, and it is without end. The more you know and understand where your company is going, what changes and challenges are happening in the industry and what the competition is doing, then the more equipped you'll be and the more confidence you'll have when you want to make your move. You don't have to know exactly what your move will be, but what you do know is that, at some point, you'll want to. Internally or externally, it's just the same. Information is power.

ELSA'S STORY

Elsa had decided that her next move was going to be to one of three companies, and she was crystal clear as to why. The three different companies were successful businesses, local to the area where Elsa lived and where she wanted to be based. As well as their proximity to her home, she'd honed in on these three businesses because of their commitment and contribution to local community and sourcing of local produce. It sounds almost too simple, but these three flagship businesses were a spot on fit for Elsa.

She treated the exercise of finding a senior role in one of these businesses like a mission and all but stalked the companies she'd identified as a fit for her. She did all the cross-referencing within her networks, reading up on the developments in the industries they operated in as well as the local day-to-day news they generated. She even went to events sponsored by the companies. (Events sponsored by a company you're interested in are a great way to meet people from that business or industry).

When the right role was advertised within one of the three businesses, Elsa was ready and didn't waste any time putting herself forward. She connected with key people on LinkedIn and spoke to her network more in-depth about the role and the business.

When it came to her interview, she wasn't overly confident or cocky but was very clear as to why she wanted to work for them, why she'd essentially chosen them as one of her key contenders for her next role and why she was – like them – so passionate about the region and contributing to the future success of the community. It's a very compelling case to make to a potential employer – to be clear about why them, why you and not to pussyfoot about it either. It also calms your nerves knowing you've prepared and already formed a sense of connection.

Elsa was able to say how she'd been waiting for something that felt like a fit to come up and was committed to moving to a business like theirs. It was a long and testing process, but Elsa's commitment to where she knew she wanted to be spurred her on and, she believes, ultimately got her the role.

Elsa's story will continue in further principles, but there's quite a ride from honing in on the role to actually being in post.

COURSES AND QUALIFICATIONS

Experience is the teacher of all things.'

~ JULIUS CAESAR

Now I'm the first to advocate the power of being a continuous learner. As someone once said to me "Kay, a learning machine is an earning machine." The idea of thinking that you know it all about your role or your industry is, of course, a myth. It can come from a sense of apathy, lack of effort or absence of confidence. I can't tell you how many women tell me that they've forgotten *how* to learn and how being a student horrifies them in case they're found out to be lacking in some way.

My view is to turn it on its head. Know that you want to learn, earn and contribute more; keep yourself updated with the latest developments; and add some letters after your name either relevant to your industry or more widely relevant like an MBA, MA or BSc.

Having been somewhat stale and stalled myself, my epiphany came when an ex-colleague pointed me in the direction of a coaching qualification. At that time, a coach to me was a bus that took you places. The term 'being coached' was one I'd never heard outside of the sporting arena. Clearly that has changed completely and these days I believe it's a badge of honour to refer to your coach. I have invested in my own coach since starting my business in 2006. They've changed as I've changed my focus, but it was only a short window when I didn't have a coach guiding and supporting me.

So, I'm a strong advocate for qualifications and courses to keep you learning and growing. Ask yourself about your own additional knowledge or where you think you have gaps. What would make sense to you to focus on? How would that help you? Would you ask your company to sponsor you or would you invest in yourself?

These days it's so easy to find ways to learn what you want online and I believe we owe it to ourselves to take ownership of this, rather than to be passive and wait until the company thinks you're ready or deserve it. Areas where you might look to shore up your skills and bolster your confidence could be:

o Presentation Skills

o Negotiation Skills

o Networking

- ○ Assertiveness Training

- ○ CV Crafting

- ○ Interview Confidence

- ○ Managing Conflict

- ○ Writing Skills

All of the above can be done in your private time if you decide to make it important. One of the most popular one-day events I host is focussed on presentation skills. Many women hate to present information, engage with an audience and lead a group. I've shown women how to break it down, to prepare differently and to actually *enjoy* it.

There is a word of caution, though, about courses and qualifications, which I've learned from my own experience and from the myriad of clients who've shared their stories with me. Here is that word – procrastination. The action of delaying or postponing something. "When I've got more experience I'll apply" or "When I've finished my MBA I'll be ready" or "I can only do this when I'm fully qualified" or "I need more experience before doing that" and so it can go on.

It can feel very logical stopping yourself from putting yourself out there by laying the blame on your own perceived lack of skills and experience. But here's the thing. The truth is we *do* have enough to start. I'm not suggesting you act recklessly around being qualified. I'm not suggesting you start seeing patients without going through medical school. What I am suggesting is to challenge yourself where you know you're not putting yourself forward for something or you're saying "No thanks" to opportunities which offer profile, visibility and a stretch just because you think you need more qualifications or more experience. This can be you putting things off.

I've worked with clients (not for long admittedly) who never actually put what they'd learned into action. They took the courses, learned solid strategies from me, qualified in their field and never actually put it into practice. That's delaying things and putting off being tested. It's also putting off the thrill of expansion of your skill set.

The truth is when you get yourself out there and start to find out what you know and what you need to know, it's like someone turning all the lights on for you. It makes you feel alive, aware and alert.

They say "The magic is there, just outside your comfort zone" and whoever *they* are, they're right. If you operate from a place of knowing everything or are not prepared to stretch until you think you do, you're always going to be playing a smaller, safer and less rewarding game.

Not being a reckless character myself, I truly understand the difference between arrogantly saying "Yes, of course I can do that" with no clue about how to do it and saying the same thing but knowing you know enough. That's the difference which will test you regularly so I want you to be aware of how you might prevent yourself from continually getting ready to be ready rather than actually making the rubber meet the road and getting on with it.

An aside about qualifications. I've rarely been asked about mine and the only person who's seen them outside of my husband Snowy, is Diane – our cleaner. They're no longer on the wall in my office now so no one sees them. They're for me to lean on but I don't get too tangled up about how people will want to see proof of them. It's more about how you *use* them and how you show up than the piece of paper. Just saying.

LENKA'S STORY

Lenka and I met when I spoke about business communication at the City Business Library in Central London. A bright and challenging audience member, Lenka asked great questions and I could tell there was something about her – a spark. A native of the Czech Republic, she was in London finalising her MBA, and her commitment to learn and understand was very clear.

Lenka's passion was to work with retail outlets to find them great locations and to negotiate with shopping malls to find them retailers for their units. The broking role relies on tenacity, confidence and connections. She was frustrated by the lack of leadership inside the organisation where she worked and then heard they would be disbanding the business down the line in the retail industry. She knew her cheese had moved and it was time for her to drive her bus.

Feeling fearful about deciding to start her own consultancy, Lenka started to look at how she could build her business and still work at her company. My American friends call this a 'side hustle' where you show up and fully engage with your day-to-day career responsibilities while learning about and planning towards something else.

Instead of thinking 'Right, I have to stop this completely, figure out what is next and then start towards that', you do things consecutively. What I like about the side hustle is that it doesn't have to feel like such an enormous step and stake-in-the-sand decision.

It does come with a price, of course. Deciding where to find and carve out that time to focus on your side hustle requires discipline and making a decision. As I say, 'Whatever you say yes to, you're already saying no to something else by definition'.

Lenka found herself getting ready to be ready when someone said, 'You're already ready. Can you consult for me now?' So, Lenka got going. She incorporated her company, found an assistant, worked out the legal ramifications and said 'Yes' before she was ready.

What Lenka's story reminded me about was that you don't have to have it all set up and shiny, worked out and ready before you get going. The piece of business would have gone elsewhere if she'd flailed about making excuses as to why she couldn't work with this potential client when, in fact, she found she could.

Another aside about qualifications is that we, as the qualified person, put much more import on the qualifications we have than others do. Now I know in a medical, plumbing or electrical capacity, it's a given that the person is qualified in the area we're wanting service. In the same way, your clients and potential employers will also assume you're qualified for the job by virtue of you putting yourself forward for the opportunity.

My point is not to lead with your qualifications. They're just a marker of your studies and commitment to your craft. Lead with what you'll be able to do for the person or organisation, what your qualifications *really* mean and how you apply them. So what if you've got an MBA from Cranfield or Harvard? If you can't demonstrate and apply skills, experience, discipline and turn them into a value-add for another entity, well, so what?

THE LANGUAGE AND LINGO OF THE INDUSTRY

'The finest language is mostly made up of simple unimposing words.'

~ *GEORGE ELIOT (MARY ANNE EVANS)*

There are two important concepts about language I want to share with you. First, be careful to make sure you express yourself clearly in a language you and others understand. Second, every industry has words, abbreviations, phrases and slang, which you must study carefully.

It's easy to get lulled into the lingo of abbreviations and forget what things actually mean. When you're new in the firm, don't just assume you understand what's meant by these terms. Ask, ask and double-check. When you've been around a while, sometimes say them out loud in full to remind both yourself and whom you're speaking with.

I recommend a number of ways to familiarise and sense-check terms, abbreviations and titles both while you're in post and when you're looking to move. Find someone you know or can trust and literally have a working list of things to ask them about – abbreviations, terms, what they mean in the context of the role and how they're applied. Sense-check them and ensure you're using them enough but not all of the time.

Research technical terms via websites, industry magazines and materials, conferences and events where you become something of a bloodhound on the scent of things you don't fully understand. Get yourself clearer and don't hesitate to ask for help.

There are a myriad of sites which will help you understand more fully the language, terminology, abbreviations and key phrases used in your industry or the industry you may be choosing to transition to.

There's nothing more dreary than listening to someone speaking in a catalogue of corporate abbreviations, which confuse and often exclude the listener. Try to use abbreviations sparingly as they lose the impact of the meaning.

One of the recent trends I've noticed is referring to Maternity Leave as 'Mat Leave'. Mat leave? One of the biggest changes in a woman's life happens the day she becomes a mother. Maternity is the phrase for the motherhood phase up to and after the birth. When you allow 'Mat Leave' to be the time you're taking away from your work, it downgrades it. The sense of the importance of it is diminished. When I hear it, I don't think of the importance of that time in the same way as I know it truly is. Not being a mother myself, I can't comment from a position of experience but I have experienced enough friends, family and clients adjusting to their new, forever, lives and being stunned at how different they feel about just about everything. Including, and often, particularly their jobs. Another abbreviation relevant here more and more in use I've noticed is a KIT Day. A Keep-In-Touch Day as part of Maternity Leave. Again, I recommend saying it in full. It diminishes the importance and significance of having this opportunity. More on this later in the book.

Someone who understands corporate terminology but doesn't use it to the exclusion of real world language is easier and more interesting to listen to, gets quicker responses and doesn't alienate people by either misunderstanding or lack of understanding. A great phrase is 'in other words' which acts like a bridge for you to transition from the corporate terminology to real world language.

For example, 'Our heavy compliance burden is costing us dearly which, in other words, means all the systems we have to put in place to keep the regulators happy and off our backs, are eating into our budgets.' Or 'When the KPIs are aligned, it will work more efficiently which, in other words, means when we agree how we'll measure the work and how it's actually working, we'll be better able to make decisions based on that information.'

The essence is to understand the language of the business you're in or want to be in. Get behind it and the meanings rather than the surface-level understanding so many operate at and be smart enough to translate it when you're trying to engage and influence others.

UNDERSTANDING TITLES

Another important aspect of using language in the best way is to understand titles and their context within a specific organization as well as the industry. See if you can find organisational charts of where you are currently and test yourself to understand exactly what each key role in the C-Suite does. What does it really entail? What are the responsibilities and the areas which report to that person? Understand as far as you can what challenges are currently facing that role and what your competitors are doing in that role.

This isn't idle internet surfing as much as it's you building up a profile; a fuller picture and deeper understanding of the way the business works currently – who's who in the zoo.

When, for example, you realise that the chief information officer is ultimately responsible for all the systems, analytics, data and the continued updating of such resources as well as the compliance of such systems with data protection, you can see how your work fits into the bigger picture.

You then can research more deeply – it took three Google clicks for me to find out that the CIO and the CMO (chief marketing officer) should be inextricably linked by what they do. Marketing relies on data and understanding who and what clients do, want and need, and how they behave. Information technology gathers this information for a purpose, one of which is marketing.

When you understand more fully the cross-pollination of such roles at the senior level and get inside some of the terminology which is commonly used (and often used to confuse), then you automatically have a wider understanding of where you fit in and, crucially, where you might add further value. A couple of useful questions for you to ask are: "What is it that I do which feeds into the bigger picture of my organisation or industry?" and "What happens to what I do when I've done it and why is it important?"

CATHERINE'S STORY

When I started working with Catherine, she described herself as something of a 'bull in a china shop'. She was an imposing woman in charge of a local social services initiative focussed on raising awareness about domestic violence. As someone working with women in the community who were either being violently abused at home or who were at risk of it, Catherine was passionate about the responsibility the council, trust, police and wider community had to protect women and their children from abusers.

I was asked to support Catherine in adjusting her style from someone who was likely to explode with frustration if she didn't feel heard or understood to someone less spiky and more strategic. She'd alienated a number of key people in her working sphere by being too forceful.

We agreed it was a delicate dance between caring and being fully committed to her cause and not taking enough into account when other people's commitment was less or their information and understanding patchy. Instead of her habit of piling in with her opinion, Catherine was working on the principle of 'seek first to understand before being understood' which is Habit 5 of Steven Covey's inspirational book, *The 7 Habits of Highly Effective People.*

Catherine was both excited and a little anxious. She'd negotiated the opportunity to speak in front of a large group of local nurses who worked in doctor's surgeries, local clinics and healthcare drop-in services and who would often be the first person to see a woman who might have signs of physical abuse. She prepared her presentation and decided to use some impactful photographs and statistics. She also planned to ask the audience lots of questions in breakout groups which is a less confronting and a more inclusive way to gather people around a subject.

The shocker came when one of the nurses responded to the first question which was along the lines of 'What experience have you had or believe you've had, of domestic violence?' She gasped and said to Catherine 'Domestic violence? I was told today was a talk about DV and I understand DV as diarrhoea and vomiting.'

This story is a quick demonstration of the huge gulf in

understanding that a simple and common abbreviation caused. Catherine managed to breathe and keep going that day, rather than have another blow out of frustration about the lack of understanding. Instead, she acknowledged how that could have happened, reassured the nurse that she'd learn something which would help her support women and families in the community and, crucially, she took this example and told her boss, the council representatives and her police contacts about it.

During the course of our work, Catherine realised there was another way to get her point across, to get people to buy into what she wanted. Like me, she was tall and fairly imposing. Instead of putting people's backs up or silencing them, she was able to use more persuasive language, draw upon the influence of others and use it for her case, and count to 10 before responding or biting back. She also took up exercise as a vent for her frustration and started open-water swimming whilst listening to the playback of our coaching calls on her waterproof iPod. Now that's maximising your time and opportunities.

JOB ADS, WHAT ATTRACTS YOU AND SKILLS THEY SEEK

Any fool can make things bigger, more complex, and more violent. It takes a touch of genius – and a lot more courage – to move in the opposite direction.'

~ALBERT EINSTEIN

It's been proven that men will apply for a role when they believe they have about 20 to 30 percent of the skills and experience required. Women, on the other hand, are far more hesitant and conservative. We feel we must wait until we have at least 85 to 100 percent of the skills or experience. I've lost count of the number of clients who avoid putting themselves forward or, if encouraged by a colleague or their boss to go for a new role, will shy away saying they don't believe they're experienced, skilled, old enough – or all three.

Knowing this, I want to encourage you to be really attentive to how you respond to the advertisements you read and what you say to yourself as you read them. "I'd love to do that but I'm not sure if I'm qualified enough yet" or "This sounds like a more senior role than I'm ready for" or "One day I'd love to do that but in a few years" and so it goes on.

I get you don't want to put yourself in a position where you feel as if you're drowning and too out of your depth. But here's the thing. When you wait to be ready or when you think you know it all or more than enough, the chances are the role won't fulfil you for long or the opportunity will have gone.

When you read through job advertisements, it's about looking for what you can do, what you've already done, what you know you're good at, where you think you can learn as you go and where you can ask for support and training. It's not about knowing it all already.

We get put off if we think we might be found wanting when instead, we need to put – as I often say – our Big Girl Pants on and trust ourselves more. Also, let's not get put off with what can sometimes be 'macho' language – a go-getter, a ninja salesperson or a power connector – expressions we don't relate to as women. We can filter these words out and translate them into a self-starter, a great salesperson, and natural relationship builder – and apply.

You'll often find your boss or your colleague will be persuading you to apply or telling you "I want you to apply for this" because they know you're ready or can get ready while doing the job. Clients tell me that they've hesitated or backed away because they don't think they're experienced enough and the job advertisement scares them or makes them worry they'll look foolish in the interview process. There is, however, a way through this and let me show you what I mean.

CHRISTINE'S STORY

I noticed Christine sitting quite close to the front at one of my three-day live events. The event content took women through various processes to encourage, inspire and dare them to step up at work and to take a chance on themselves and their potential, rather than let others keep overtaking them.

Noticing her looking very serious and, if I'm honest, giving the air of being really fed up, I kept reminding myself that you can't please everyone all of the time and that she could always leave if she was *that* fed up. It's interesting, isn't it, how we assume things are about us and not about the other person? That's what I'd done in that moment by thinking it was about my content, and I know better than to assume that.

After bringing the event to a close, I love to have my photo taken with women who want to come on stage and celebrate all that has happened for them over the three days. I spotted Christine coming towards me on the stage, still with that face which didn't really tell me what she was feeling. I sensed something was about to open up.

In the moment we came face to face, Christine threw herself into my arms and began sobbing: "I've been so shaken up these three days, Kay. I have wanted to burst into tears, jump about in frustration and just swear and curse."

She explained to me that she'd felt for years as if she should leave her current role and take all her experience working for the National Health Service in the UK and instead work for one of the major cancer charities.

Her passion and mission in life was to support patients with cancer and to add weight to the research and development of treatment for the disease.

She was stuck, frustrated and feeling as if she was spinning her wheels where she was with little to no prospect of advancement. You may sense this in your own role and know deep down that what got you to where you are now isn't enough or isn't a fit to get you where you want to go anymore.

In that moment, Christine told me she was going to take action. She didn't know exactly what, but that she was going to use all she'd learned about herself from the exercises, discussions, audience stories and her sense of frustration to channel into finding a new role. Okay then. *Now* I understood why she'd looked so deep in thought and so fed up.

She made me laugh because I commented on how I'd assumed she was borderline bored throughout the event. She said "Oh Kay, I just have an RBF – Resting Bitch Face. When I'm deep in thought, I look fed up". So many lessons for us both in that moment.

So, what did she do next and how does it relate to job advertisements and you? About three months later, I received a card in the post from Christine with a picture of a dog wearing flying goggles with the caption 'Great Expectations' next to it. Not only had Christine found herself a new role and was about to start, but she had a strong, compelling story about what actually happened.

After the event, she was so fired up to take action and stop second-guessing her instincts that she knocked her CV into shape and applied for a role she'd seen advertised which she had not felt confident enough to apply for before. It was working for one of the UK's biggest and most influential cancer charities. Even though the deadline date for applications had closed, Christine sent in her CV anyway with a heartfelt, compelling covering letter asking to be considered if the role hadn't been filled.

It hadn't been filled. Christine was quickly interviewed

and offered the role. Here's the even sweeter spot for you to know. Because of how well she interviewed and how much they wanted her, Christine negotiated her salary with them. The salary on offer was what she was already earning and so, with a deep breath and building on her newfound confidence, Christine negotiated a higher amount, which would work for her and for the organisation.

It makes me emotional just writing this because it proves how easy it is to assume things are too late or will inconvenience someone if you take action when, in fact, invariably it's the opposite. The organisation would have missed out on the brilliance of Christine's experience and wisdom, and she herself would have been kicking herself that she'd missed out on that opportunity. It does remind me of that phrase 'It's not over until it's over and, even then, it's not over'.

Remember Christine's story as you look at job advertisements and assume you can't; it's too late; or it's too *something* for you. Maybe it isn't and maybe, by putting yourself forward, you are invited to consider another role. Maybe one that's even better. The key is to be in the game, isn't it? Not to be watching, waiting and hoping from the sidelines. Christine put herself firmly into the game, and it's now my hope that her story helps you to do the same too.

SNAKES & THE CORPORATE LATTICE

'The secret of change is to focus all of your energy, not on fighting the old, but on building the new.'

~SOCRATES

For the most part, the whole corporate ladder construct has shifted beyond recognition with flatter management structures and less clear and incremental career moves. With remote working, working from home, virtual teams, job-sharing, outsourcing, off-shore resourcing, robotics, artificial intelligence and a myriad of ways we work, it shows how murky the working career path is and how prolific the opportunities actually are. It's a sign of the times and one that we must be savvy about and comfortable working with.

The whole 'job for life' concept, which my father certainly had when he started working for the firm where I also worked, has long gone. Mergers, takeovers, buyouts, restructures and right-sizing (management speak for redundancies) have changed the shape of both our expectations and loyalties and, quite naturally, the path ahead. It's no longer a ladder where you worked for so many years and then could expect a natural next move upwards to the role on the rung above you, as long as you stayed or were not worn down by the competition.

Your promotions at work may have felt a little like the game of Snakes & Ladders, where the principle is that you keep moving with the random throw of the dice. You gradually move forward or come cross a ladder to climb up and jump ahead or, at times, land on a snake, slide down and move backwards as a result.

Today we can talk about navigating the corporate *lattice* instead. I first heard the expression 'corporate lattice' from one of my American friends. As Cathy Benko wrote in her

2010 article in the *Harvard Business Review* entitled 'How The Corporate Ladder Became The Corporate Lattice'.

"In mathematics, a lattice is a multi-dimensional structure that extends infinitely in any direction. A trellis is a garden-variety example. A lattice is an adaptive construct chock full of options so if you imagine a lattice structure in the wider scheme of your working life, you'll start to see many more options and possibilities where before you may not have noticed or given any focus."

So, what might be possible if you adapted the corporate lattice mindset instead?

o Could you work from your home office and be as, if not more, effective?

o Could you get involved in work on other time zones, which would work better for you and your home life?

o Could you discuss compressed hours where you work your core hours in four rather than five days?

o What do you love to do in your role, which, if you could choose, you'd do more and more?

o How could that skill or set of skills be repositioned or showcased inside your organisation?

o If they can't as far as you can see, who do you know who could give you a lead-in to somewhere else?

o What if you looked at job-sharing so you can marry your lifestyle with your work life to give you more balance?

○ Maybe some of the automation or offshore working which has been introduced could lead to redundancy for you and maybe your company encourages voluntary redundancy. How could you find out and give yourself a buffer of time and money?

○ When you look at what your area is struggling with or where time is being sucked, how could you add value and get involved in the solution for this?

○ Knowing that women are as much joint breadwinners as often the primary breadwinner and that a marriage is no longer the forever after career move it was for my mother (nowadays, the marriage doesn't always last and/or nor does the husband's career trajectory) how can you look at equal opportunities and diversity initiatives and take advantage of them?

○ How could you take a sideways move to another area and then gain momentum from there by benefitting from the focus or structure there?

○ Where could you take a chance on yourself by seeing where the company is going and put yourself forward to either innovate or be part of a project innovating or fixing an old problem?

I know the above questions are general ones because this book is designed to be universally useful to corporate career women wherever you are in your career cycle.

My intention is to give you a place to find yourself if you sense that your cheese has moved and the path ahead isn't straightforward. What I do know is that the future is packed with opportunities for you if you look closely enough.

HELEN'S STORY

When Helen first joined my Mastermind mentoring group, The VIP Golden Circle, she wrote in her application that she knew a big change was coming in her industry and thought it likely that she'd be made redundant in around eighteen months. That's quite a thought to wrestle with as you continue to go for it day-to-day in a demanding role, yet you also know that there's a juggernaut of change heading towards you.

It's in these kinds of circumstances that you have the opportunity to really shake things up in your life. It requires a state of mind which is flexible, open to change and adaptable to thinking differently about what you want to do next or for the next chapter.

Let's be honest. If you're reading this and are in your late 30s to early 40s – which many of my clients are – you're looking ahead to at least another 20 to 30 more working years. This isn't to horrify you as much as it is to inspire you to make sure that you do work you're good at, with people you like and find rewards both financially and morally that satisfy you. It's a long old haul otherwise.

So, Helen decided to stay the distance and look at what opportunities presented themselves inside her organisation in the lead-up to her team being disbanded as well. She also kept her eye on the possibility that she might just navigate towards the redundancy route and give herself a break after 18 years of full-time working.

It's an inspiring, exciting and scary situation to find yourself in and one which can threaten to overwhelm you with self-doubt and fear if you're not paying close attention to what's going on around you and understanding more fully what makes you tick. It's easy to get swept along with everyone saying 'Oh Helen, what are you going to do next?' and 'Are you looking for a new role yet?' and a lot of fear-based fretting which, as I always say, gives you the permission to respond with 'Hmmm, it depends.' It depends on many things, and Helen taught us in our group to play with your own cards – the cards you've been dealt and not the ones everyone else is playing with.

Having worked for the same organisation for such a long time, she knew her way around and knew many people who knew her. She'd grown and developed a successful team concentrating on a certain area of the business, which gave her credibility to leverage as the wave of change approached.

But here's the thing. It's easy to assume you have to do what's expected of you. What was expected of Helen was to quickly find another role by either applying for the various roles available inside the newly-merged organisation or to get her skates on and start applying for external roles.

What Helen did was different and a great example of

thinking of your career more as a lattice than a ladder. She got her CV up to date. We made sure that, even though she'd been in the same organisation for a long time, the various roles she'd taken on, the value she'd added and the progression she'd made were clearly showcased It wasn't just a list; it was a compelling story.

As the time approached when Helen's team would be disbanded and the organisation would absorb their responsibilities at an overseas location, she sensed that rather than jump into a role which felt alright but didn't excite or scare her, she might need to put the brakes on and give herself a break. It was a calculated gamble she decided to take. She felt full of the emotion of what was happening around her and also tired and drained. This wasn't an energy she wanted to be leading her new role search with.

Helen took the redundancy option, which allowed her to play with her own cards rather than allowing everyone else's situation to influence hers. She realised she could have her first ever extended break in 18 years to travel and do some home improvements. She gave herself the gift of time to consider what she really wanted to do rather than what she felt she ought to do.

That's my definition of playing with your own cards. She didn't have a family to consider. She was a free agent to decide if working in the same way and at the same pace suited her. That's a big difference and I know you'll know this if you've ever looked around and thought 'You know what, I don't have to do this or that, I can do something else instead'.

Having six months off after negotiating and accepting the redundancy package, Helen was approached via an ex-colleague to look at a lattice-type move. A small, start-up, family firm wanted someone who had great people skills and who'd navigated change inside a big corporate. They wanted a self-starter who could work with their clients to introduce and manage change inside their organisations.

Helen has had challenges adjusting to her new role. She's now the agent rather than the client. She has no team to lead. So, the jury is still out. But the lattice way of working – of looking more widely at your skills, at what's out there and what suits you and your lifestyle now – is crucial to seeing and investigating possibilities where others see roadblocks.

Diana Ross was the member of The Supremes who had the longest and most successful career of her band members and is remembered personally rather than as 'just one of the band'. She said it well: "You can't just sit there and wait for people to give you that golden dream, you've got to get out there and make it happen for yourself."

She's right. The lattice will help you think more broadly about where you want to go next. Now, let's move on to **Principle 3** in Your Career Success Cycle™ and that's **Prepare, Plot, Plan (and Keep Going).** So, let's go.

*'There is no such thing as a career path.
There is only crazy paving and you have to lay it
yourself.'*

- SIR DOMINIC CADBURY

"For tomorrow belongs to the people who prepare for it today."

– AFRICAN PROVERB

PRINCIPLE 3:

PREPARE, PLOT, PLAN (& KEEP GOING)

Getting ready to get ready is procrastination. If you know you're guilty of constantly preparing, researching, qualifying, training and wondering, then this is a wake-up call Principle for you.

One of the fastest paths to your success and your next move is *being* ready to be ready. Your Career Success Cycle™ relies on you getting your ducks in a row and then keeping them in a row. That means keeping things up-to-date and not becoming complacent. Getting ready to take action and being ready to say "yes" to opportunity as it presents itself is what I'm talking about.

BE CV-READY (AND EVER-READY)

'Luck is what happens when preparation meets opportunity'

~ SENECA

It's easy to assume you don't need to have a CV (Resumé), or you don't need to keep the one that you have sharp and up-to-date. Easy, but not wise. You may think that it's not the best investment of your limited time if you have a fulfilling career. Dedicating the time to showcasing yourself on paper or on LinkedIn, for example, may simply seem unnecessary.

Here's the thing I've learned from my work with thousands of corporate career women and from being one myself. We tend to focus on where we are and invest ourselves fully in the now and not, as a rule, look more widely at what's next. We are often more passive than is good for us and this is where I want to encourage you to be 'ever ready' and to future-proof your career moves as you do.

I want you to be ready for change in whatever shape or form it comes to you and be ready to showcase yourself with your career history carefully thought out. I want you to avoid the scramble for time and have the confidence to put yourself out there on paper when opportunity comes knocking or when your circumstances change.

The first part is understanding that your career path is always subject to change, forks in the road and twists and turns in opportunity, needs, health and focus. You never know when your personal circumstances will require you to change direction.

Maybe your husband or partner's role, health or ability to earn will challenge your family lifestyle. Maybe your relationship will falter and suddenly, two incomes is just one – yours. Maybe you will combine forces with your partner and then suddenly your income increases and one of you wants to change the pace and focus, just like I did. Maybe your role will shrink or not inspire you anymore; you will know it's time to take your skills and experience elsewhere before you go mad. There are a myriad of possibilities that can challenge your status quo and they can happen quickly.

Having an up-to-date and clearly laid out CV is a key part of being able to confidently and quickly respond to these ever-changing circumstances. For several years, I've hosted a Strategic Saturday CV Surgery to bring women together so they can work with each other and me to bring their CV to life in just a day. Either from scratch or through editing and polishing the one they already have, the CV they go on to create is both challenging and inspiring. I've proved to myself each time that those who perform 'surgery' on their CVs seem to attract opportunities to themselves just by doing this work. So, of course, can you.

While I'm not going to try to give you all the nuts and bolts of creating a CV, I've learned some really helpful tips from a talent acquisition expert who shared with me the pitfalls to avoid and key actions to take as well as a suggested outline.

You can find more in-depth information to download at **www. kaywhite.com/bookresources**

Here are a few key headlines for you.

- **Keep your CV to two pages maximum**. You can always add a summary sheet or additional information sheet connected to a particular role but keep the actual CV itself to two pages.

- **Make your first page punchy and clear**. Most people don't get past the first page before they decide if they want to see you or not.

- **Include a personal statement**. Underneath your name and contact details, the first thing I suggest is your personal statement that describes you and the kind of person you are, what makes you tick and why you should be considered for the role.

- **Modify each time you go for a role.** One size does not fit all. Really, it doesn't. When you're looking at the opportunity you're going for or the organisation you're in discussions with, you must consider the language of the role and of the industry. Where can you bring out certain skills more clearly or showcase experience you've had which appears relevant to the role? I recommend having a master CV and then tailoring the master to *each* approach or opportunity.

- **Update it annually.** This might sound like hard work to you, but here's the thing. When someone asks you to drop him or her a note with your CV because they were talking about you or know someone who's already interested in you – yes, this happens a lot – you don't want to be scrambling for your information. Once you've got your CV updated, keep it that way. It's a date in your diary, for example, just after your appraisal. It's up to you to commit to doing this for yourself and I *really* recommend it as a habit.

- **Invite feedback before you go out with it.** It sounds so obvious, but you must ask someone else to read your CV not only to sense-check it, but also to have someone else's eyes, ears and opinions on it. It's so easy to repeat yourself, to lose track of the point you're trying to make, or to underplay your skills and value (more on that later).

- **Use your CV in multiple ways.** Yes, there's a bonus to all of this. Your updated CV will shape your LinkedIn profile (you do have one don't you?), and you can take pieces and add them to internal biographies, event profiles and intranet profiles. The key is to have it in one place first.

- **Make your LinkedIn profile punchy and working for you.** With your CV updated, you can then go in and make the most of the 24/7 working of LinkedIn. I've lost track of the number of clients who've been approached via LinkedIn. Keeping yourself visible, updated and punchy on LinkedIn is key and all part of the cycle. Every time you add a new title and qualify or take part in something, remember to update LinkedIn at the same time. Choose to let your connections see your updates, which is a great way to pop up on their radar.

○ **Think of your CV as your shop window.** Consider how shops draw you in from your busy life and encourage you into the store. The shop window needs to be compelling, attractive, clearly demonstrating value and offering the kind of things you want. Your CV is meant to do these exact things too. Your experience, skills, qualifications and interests will speak for you long before you have a chance to. Your shop window needs to clearly point towards what you'll be able to bring to a role or organisation.

Here are the key components of your CV to get you going and let me give you 10 impactful Action Verb examples for you to use to beef it up. Find these as part of your PowerPack resources at **www.kaywhite.com/bookresources** and finish the sentence using these kind of verbs.

○ **Personal Statement** – as described above

○ **Key Skills & Achievements** – a summary of the types of skills you have and how you've applied them

○ **Roles & Responsibilities** – reversing from the current date, your career history and what you did/added/made happen

- **Education & Qualifications** – both professional and personal qualifications starting with the most recent

- **Personal Interests** – an area so often underestimated and so important. What is it that you do when you're not working? Don't just put 'reading'. Put the kind of books you enjoy and the most recent book you read and why you loved it. You get the idea. It's a place to showcase your wider life interests and is often the hook that can get you the first interview. When you take the time to do this exercise for yourself, you'll find just how useful the content is and be prepared to have approaches. It's as if invisible forces conspire to reward you for doing this work. And remember, you're *already* ready for it, even if you don't think you are. Once you see yourself as being in this continuous cycle, then it will make it easier for you to keep going and to keep an eye on how the things you already do or know can be applied to make yourself more portable, transferrable and marketable.

DAWN'S STORY

Dawn realised after we completed the process of creating a strong, compelling CV for her that she had real 'walkability'. She got the sense that her clearly summarised skills and experience were both valuable and needed. It was not always this way.

When Dawn heard me speak at a networking meeting for senior London women, she just knew it was time to take action and drive her career bus. She was frustrated and stuck, stagnant and bored, and didn't know how to change things.

She'd been involved in more restructures in the last couple of years than she could actually remember, and those key people who knew her and understood her skill set had been restructured themselves. It's easy to fall through the cracks in this kind of scenario and this is where having the mentality of being at the wheel of your own career bus gives you the awareness and know-how to take action.

Dawn and I decided to work together in an intensive, 90-day private mentorship. During that time, as well as looking at wider opportunities both in the bank where she worked as well as externally, we would create Dawn's CV using resources, action verbs, templates and guided questions to draw out and organise her experience.

One of the most surprising things I discovered when Dawn sent me the first draft of her CV was her name with PhD by the side of it. Dawn had a PhD in Biochemistry. Now while this wasn't necessarily a qualification needed to be a successful finance director in a bank, it spoke volumes about her experience, dedication, and commitment plus her ability to research problems and write up analytics from the data.

When Dawn started to look more widely at who's who in her network (more on this in Principle 4, Leverage Your Connections) and how she was now talking about herself, it boosted her confidence. Seeing her experience laid out in a punchy, two-page document gave her – and anyone she showed it to – a sense of just how experienced she was and where she could really add value.

She focussed on the savings she'd made for the businesses she worked for, specifically the amount of time saved by creating strict processes, which kept the business compliant and on the right side of the regulators while still having a commercial edge. All these attributes and achievements gave Dawn a sense of just how much she had to offer and how much she'd let herself slip into a rut where she didn't use these skills or, when she did, she didn't understand what they were doing.

What I know to be true in Dawn's case is that she wasn't going to attract another role unless she really reconnected herself with the value she added and the way she was able to add to the business bottom line. We did a number of exercises, which encouraged her to give rock solid examples of these kinds of results. I'm going to show you a little of what we did later in this Principle.

As a result of investing and putting herself out there, Dawn attracted three solid new role offers. Her initial approach for the role she finally took was via LinkedIn and an ex-colleague. As an aside, Dawn was sought out via LinkedIn for another role, by a recruitment agent. Although that role didn't suit, the recruitment agent arranged a speculative coffee and chat with the CFO of the company she eventually went to work for. At the time there was no specific role, but a reorganisation within the team created an opportunity. Doesn't Dawn's story just show you how you must get out there and have these conversations? Her CV was all ready to go and her LinkedIn profile opened the door. There was a point when Dawn had accepted her new role and, even though she told another company who was interested in her that she'd already accepted an offer, they really encouraged her to meet them 'just in case.' So, she did.

For me that was such a smart move. You never know what will come from that meeting, who will remember you for something else, and who you can help with your own recommendations. Rather than the easy 'No thanks, I'm already going to work for ABC Company' it's more a case of 'Yes, let's have a coffee, I'm always open to looking at if or how I can help and who knows what the future holds' kind of approach. Open, engaging and very smart. Just like Dawn.

The key lesson here is to invest the time to intentionally craft an interview and opportunity attracting CV, which speaks for you about the value and experience you already have and the potential value you'll bring. Not just a list of tasks.

ALEXANDRA'S STORY

After investing time and energy in participating in my one-day CV Surgery workshop, Alexandra set to work on her CV. She knew she was ready to take on more responsibility and scope in her current role and prepping her CV was as much about reconnecting with her skills and experience as it was about considering taking them elsewhere. When I reviewed Alexandra's CV, it was very impressive. It showed the depth of her knowledge, ability to lead, tenacity with large projects and trustworthiness in keeping on the right side of the regulators in her part of the bank. During her next one-to-one with her boss, Alexandra told him she'd invested in herself and worked with someone on her CV and got it to a stage where she was really pleased with it. She explained she wanted more responsibility and scope for promotion and development where she was and wanted to stay. She also said she was prepared now to look in the wider industry.

Here is the short version of the response Alexandra received – a 25% salary increase plus more responsibilities and scope within her current role, which stretch and excite her. It was such a smart thing to do, having a conversation that involves and informs, rather than threatens the other person. In this case, Alexandra's boss and her response shows the depth of the commitment to both retaining her and keeping her developing. Win. Win.

HOW YOU SPEAK ABOUT YOURSELF

'If you don't toot your own horn,
don't complain that there's no music.'

~ GUY KAWASAKI

When you consider what a promotion or new opportunity you're tempted with might look like, the first thing that often comes to many brilliant women is "Oh my goodness, I'd have to interview and talk about myself and I hate that." Well, what if I was to tell you that there is a way to do this – one I do all the time myself from the stage when I'm speaking to groups – which feels natural and of service to the other person or group?

Here's the thing. We *want* you to be good. We want to know you're an expert or have expertise in a certain area if we're going to consider you, listen to you, buy from you, interview you or employ you. You get the idea. You owe it to yourself to be able to offer the person or persons you're seeking to influence a simple grasp of why they should consider you.

When I speak, I tell my audience that I'm a number one best-selling author; run a multiple six figure business from my home; mentor career women; show them how to get promoted without selling their souls; and demonstrate how to negotiate and get paid more money. All of these things are true, *and* I say it in a certain way. This is what I want to encourage you to learn to do so people will listen to you when you showcase your experience and why you should be considered.

If you learn to turn your 'toot' – which could be along the lines of 'I'm able to turn projects going off track around and bring them in on time and under budget' – into a concise, outcome-filled story, then you're more compelling and don't come off as blowing your own trumpet. You're simply giving information and examples. Here's how it could sound: 'I'm able to turn projects going off track around and bring them in on time and under budget. When I was brought–manage the ABC Project, it was already behind the projected deadline because of team members leaving due to lack of direction. Expenses were out of control due to lack of attention. The project was crucial to the risk and compliance initiatives of the business and we had to respond to the regulator's strict guidelines. I quickly identified X, brought the situation to the attention of Y, introduced tighter reporting lines on Z and negotiated a short extension with the regulator. We brought the project in within the new deadline and overall saved 15%.'

This example, of course, is fictitious, and you will have your own outcome, action-driven stories that speak for your expertise. The important thing is to pay attention to the *structure* since it helps you weed out the detail and explanations, which can take away the punch from your story. The structure I want to introduce you to is called the STAR Model. I can't find reference to who first identified it but it's brilliant because it's simple and easy to remember.

THE STAR MODEL

The STAR Model enables you to tell a story within a structure to keep you on point and enable you to toot your horn without blowing your own trumpet. Once your CV is knocked into shape, you'll want to be clear about examples from your experience, which demonstrate your skills. STAR helps you do just that.

S – Situation – What has happened? What was the context of how you were involved? Why was it important?

T – Task – What did you have to do or get involved in? How did you use your skills?

A – Actions – What did you do, make happen, introduce or decide?

R – Results – How did it all end up? What did you do, save and generate? What difference did it make?

Let's take one of my examples and use STAR to turn it into a punchy and true story – *'I'm a number one best-selling author.'*

Situation: I knew it was time to write down some of what I knew. So many people had been asking me where they could find out more of what I was sharing about communication strategies and choosing strong words to get your point across.

Task: The idea for my first book, *The A to Z of Being Understood*, came to me on a plane flying across the Atlantic. I jotted out A, B, C etc. all the way down a page and immediately filled out the 26 lessons each letter represented. I knew in that moment exactly what they were, but how was I going to actually write it?

Actions: I decided to invest in a book mentor to guide me and keep me on track. I got up at 5 a.m. and wrote most mornings for an hour. Even though I struggled with self-doubt at times, it took eight months from the time I had the idea to having the book in my hand on stage at an event.

Results: The book became a number one bestseller when it was released and shortly after its release, it was taught to MBA students in Austria. It all came from taking that action in the moment, investing in others' expertise and daring myself to do something I didn't think I could. It wasn't always easy, but I committed and kept going.

The bonus with this model is that it's easy to remember, so on the fly, you can keep yourself in check by mentally filling in these prompts. Situation. Task. Actions. Results. You also don't need everything perfectly neat and exactly in the order, although the order does help the punch of your story.

STAR will enable you to put yourself forward and effectively choose yourself to showcase, rather than deflect your experience and wisdom on to others and leave yourself out. It's not fair to you and it's not fair to your team and family. We want you to show your brilliance, and we want you to be rewarded for it too.

It's good to put your feet to the flames to own your brilliance and what you'll be able to do for someone. From here you can negotiate more for yourself (more on that later in this book) and your self-esteem and self-belief rise along with your profile.

Try reverse engineering some of your achievements into STAR and then speak it out to a trusted friend or colleague. They don't have to know what you're doing but watch for their reaction. It will surprise you. Toot. Toot.

THE FABB VERSION OF YOU: HOW TO SPEAK OF YOUR VALUE

'We don't get paid for the hour, we get paid for the value we bring to the hour.'

~ JIM ROHN

In the previous section, I gave you a model to help frame your story in an engaging way that shows how your achievements can benefit others. However, if you do not understand and know your value, this can be difficult to do.

This is a really sticky point for so many people, men and women alike – but particularly for women: how to understand and own the value you add, where to find it and when you do, how to talk about it.

I use another structure like STAR to help women find the value of what they do. The distinction I want for you to understand is that you're not paid for what you actually do. You're paid for the *value* of what you do – what 'what you do' *does*.

I've listened to women on the brink of frustrated outbursts at work saying things like "But Kay I've worked so hard and built the team up and kept our headcount turnover low and all the other things I'm supposed to do and no one really acknowledges it" or "I show up and do all my work and those floorwalkers, those people who don't work nearly as hard as me, they seem to get all the opportunities."

There is no surprise here because these women are describing what they actually do in task-driven descriptions and just how much they do of it, not what impact or difference their work makes. The key is connecting yourself and your output to the wider scope of your business or industry and understanding how the result of your work enables the business to succeed. If your accurate and timely data entries, for example, enable the trading desk to make quick and informed decisions about stocks they buy or sell, then the outcome of your work is clearer and connected to business bottom-line. This is the value. This is where you make people's ears prick up by connecting what your work *does* in the wider scope of the business.

Here's how to find your version of this magical set of words. You'll have many versions as you break down the various tasks and responsibilities you have. I learned this by studying how marketers find differentiating reasons why we should buy one product over another one.

It's called the FABB Model except marketers tend to leave out the 2nd B and that's where your version of the *real* magic is.

F is for Features. These are your qualifications, experience and years of service – the things that enable you to do your job and give you credibility in the first place.

A is for Advantages. What are the advantages of the features you have? What do you do that gives you an advantage?

B is for Benefits. What are the benefits of what you're able to do, produce, manage, avoid, and offer?

B is for the Benefits of the Benefits. What do the benefits do to help your company succeed? This is the magical piece and where your wider value is identified. This allows you to leverage your conversations about what your work actually does and contributes.

Let's put a couple of examples into the model to show you how this sounds in a workable way. If I were to use my own 'value' as I understand it and place it inside the model, it would be as follows:

Features – Over 20 years of corporate career experience working for a global insurance broker. Studied coaching and neuro linguistic programming to trainer level. Set up and started own business generating multiple six figures annually.

Advantages – Full and deep personal understanding of the challenges my clients face and the landscape in which they operate as well as a psychological set of skills to encourage them to take control of how they develop their own career prospects.

Benefits – Clients develop the confidence and certainty to be able to negotiate promotions and pay rises and comfortably discuss their contribution and leverage themselves.

Benefits of the Benefits – Women never get stuck in a role which no longer fits them; they can confidently move their career onwards because they understand the value they bring and they own it *and* they can support their family and lifestyle without selling their souls.

If you're looking at the Benefit of the Benefits to the organisation, more confident, ambitious women leaders lead to a more successful, diverse and competitive business, plus lower turnover because of unhappy, frustrated women.

The *key to* getting the Benefit of the Benefits clearly stated is you can't say "So what?" to them. You can't say "So what?" to what I've said above because everyone wants to be able to do this and once you get the value of what you offer with your work, you will too.

Let's say you're a lawyer with ten years practice experience and you've moved into insurance broking to negotiate claims handling. Here's how that could sound.

Features – Law degree and ten years practicing in a law firm, ACII qualification from the Chartered Insurance Institute with ten years' experience of claims handling and contract negotiation.

Advantages – Wide understanding of the law relating to underwriting and claims as well as day-to-day legal queries, avoiding need to engage external lawyers and legal fees.

Benefits – Colleagues and clients receive speedy advice with a commercial edge without protracted discussions with external advisors needing to be involved.

Benefits of the Benefits – The business is able to offer compliant, robust advice which gives them the edge in negotiating new business leads. The clients, in turn, have the comfort of knowing their brokers are able to respond quickly to any claims situation.

You just can't say "So what" to that either. You could say "So what" if she stopped at the advantages. It's the *depth* that gets the magic going. Everyone wants sound, quick and robust advice and for Sara, whose FABB value model this is, she has a story to share.

SARA'S STORY

'Beyond frustrated' was how Sara described herself when we first met. The rough and tumble world of insurance broking at that time made her very unhappy and this was also spilling out at home.

We had a conversation about what was going on and what the impact was for Sara and agreed to work together over the course of about six months. Sara and I looked at how she could better manage the day-to-day frustration she felt at the way her company was being run, how she was expected to work and the way information was bypassing her. She acknowledged part of this was because she'd allowed things to get worse after the organisation had experienced restructure after restructure and she felt she'd lost her sponsors – and her way.

She also decided after looking at other roles in the industry that it would be more of the same. She used the somewhat pithy phrase 'shame shit, different bucket.' What was the point of trying to move within the industry to a similar role when she felt she'd lost her mojo?

If this speaks to you in any way, you know it's a tough place to find yourself. It affects how you feel about so many other things outside of work; your self-worth, confidence and future potential get questioned. Sara and I knew it was time to find a way out before her disruptive and, at times, explosive behaviour caused some kind of performance review issue.

When Sara and I focussed on getting her CV knocked into shape from scratch, that's when the light bulb moment happened. We dug about in her past to look closely at her career path from when she started out. As her beady-eyed mentor, I noticed something I hadn't heard her mention. Sara was a qualified lawyer who'd chosen to leave private practice and move into the insurance world. She'd stopped leading with her law qualification and experience. She had kind of forgotten that it was a skill set that was being underestimated.

Rather than trying to shoehorn herself into roles that didn't excite her, Sara shifted her focus into combining her legal background with insurance. The jolt of energy and focus she got was as if she'd plugged herself into the mains. I encourage you to look closely at skills, experience and qualifications you may not be using or acknowledging when you're looking at new roles.

Through her connections, Sara found herself a role in a small, niche, start-up organisation, which services the insurance industry as outsourced lawyers. She became a specialist, giving advice on legal contracts, being their legal counsel but without fixed contracts and focusing solely on certain classes of insurance. She is now a bridge between the commercial needs of the businesses she represents from a claims perspective and the legal obligations that arise. She has the unusual skill set which combines these two key areas and that was unlikely to be written in a job advertisement.

PRESENTING YOUR BEST SELF

'Looking good isn't self-importance; it's self-respect'

~ *CHARLES HIX*

I want to speak to you about how you sparkle personally – how to physically present your best self as you put yourself forward for opportunities or respond to ones you attract. It was one of the topics of an event I hosted called Show Up, Sparkle & Be Heard.

Clearly this subject is sensitive and one that could take up the rest of this book. What I want you to ask yourself within the context of 'It's *Always* Your Move' is how comfortable are you with what you wear? What does your personal style say about you, how you think about yourself and how you present yourself at work?

It's very easy to get stuck in a style groove where you wear what you've always worn or what everyone else seems to be wearing. You're not really sure if that's what suits you best. I'm going to invite you to consider three key components to determine if you are presenting your best self.

COLOUR

One of the best investments I have ever made is having my colour analysis done. It stopped me buying pieces in colours that looked great on the person wearing it or were in fashion. It has made me switch to *only* buying things in my colour, shade and tone.

It spills out into how I chose my branding, my website and my book covers – always in colours I love which suit me. That's the key. Personalised for you. Not your mother's or best friend's favourite colours, but the ones that actually really suit *you.*

Your colour palette relates to your eye colour and skin tone which, as my own colour mentor Mandy says along the lines of, "You arrive on the planet with and leave the planet with – they don't change." If you search out colour analysis or colour and style analysis, you'll find a myriad of choices wherever you are in the world.

I'm a spring colour palette – different companies have differing ways of analysing your palette – and I immediately got the difference it made.

STYLE

Understanding your body shape – not size, but shape – is another key factor, which adds to our confidence and certainty when investing in outfits. I thought I had this piece sorted out. For 40 plus years, I'd been largely wearing what I thought suited me, but there were times when I couldn't understand why things I loved in magazines or looked great on a friend made me look like a rugby player or, to be honest, a fairy elephant.

Here's what I found out by having my style and lifestyle analysis done for a relatively small investment. I was told my shoulder width was wider than my hips and so I needed to think of myself as a triangle. Everything which just hangs off my shoulders like a loose top or kaftan kind of thing makes me look huge because it doesn't give me any shape or distinction at my waist or down below.

I now shop for V-neck dresses or jerseys. Rarely do I wear round necks because they don't draw attention away from my shoulders. My hips need fitted skirts and trousers and flare from my thighs for the same reason – to keep my shape tight around my hips.

This piece alone is a game-changer for what you choose to wear and what you choose to invest in as you decide to show up more fully. At the time of writing, let me recommend you to House of Colour and It's My Colour, two UK-based organisations I've worked with and who will make it easy for you to understand what suits you best. It's a science (rather than a whimsy) to understand your own body shape and which parts to bring attention to with colour and accessories as well as which parts to play down.

BODY LANGUAGE

A whole industry exists to encourage us to consider our body language and the effect it has on us and those we seek to influence. How you stand, breathe, make eye contact, smile and rest your arms all send subtle and influential messages. The secret bonus is how these kinds of physical moves make you feel internally and how they add to your ability to be present and *have* presence. I want to encourage you to consider three key things, which influence you and others at work.

How you hold yourself. If you know you slump when you're sitting, I encourage you to sit straighter and put your shoulders back. It affects your ability to breathe deeply into your diaphragm, which in turn affects the tone of your voice, your sense of calm and whether people think you're engaged or not. I'm not talking about being bolt upright as if you've had a fright but, rather standing and sitting to show you are paying attention and ready to participate.

When you're standing, consider whether your shoulders are back and whether you round your shoulders or droop your head. These poses speak about you before you open your mouth, and we want you to give yourself the best shot at creating a strong first impression.

How (or if) you use your space. Women tend to make themselves smaller or try to take up less space. We think it's more feminine to curl up or be tidy around ourselves at a meeting table. Particularly in an interview, making yourself smaller by folding your arms, dropping your head or playing with your neck or hair speaks volumes about how confident you feel. I want to invite you to use your space to spread out and sit forward. This is the same as when you're standing at a conference or networking event.

Fill yourself out. I don't mean you should 'manspread' – that male phenomenon of sitting with your legs wide apart to take up more room. I do mean that it's an easy fix to consciously make yourself bigger in moments that count.

How to have presence. When social psychologist, Amy Cuddy gave her TED Talk in 2012, she had no idea that she'd be creating interest and discussions about a whole new science about posture and power posing. Her talk, which I wholly recommend to you, is entitled 'Your Body Language May Shape Who You Are.' It focuses on her findings from research she leads as a Harvard University professor. The research demonstrates a significant increase in levels of confidence and ability to act by making some simple but far-reaching adjustments to body language.

The premise is that certain power poses when tested increased levels of testosterone – the confidence-boosting hormone – and decrease levels of cortisol – the anxiety-induced 'fight or flight' hormone. By shifting the balance of these, it dramatically affected the participants' ability to be comfortable, articulate and bolder in how they came across.

Her work has been associated with The Wonder Woman Pose – legs apart, hands on hips, shoulders back, head upright and forward facing. Standing like this privately for two minutes *before* one of those moments that challenge you – a tricky conversation with your boss, an interview, appraisal, or conflict-style meeting – steadies you and calms your nerves. It truly works. I know because I do it all the time myself and I really encourage you to find a moment in a private space and try it for yourself.

We'll refer to this piece of science later in **Principle 5: Shine In Interviews & Appraisals** but, for now, let me encourage you to watch Amy Cuddy's TED talk or to invest in her book *Presence: Bringing Your Boldest Self to Your Biggest Challenges*.

OLIVIA'S STORY

Olivia had just been promoted with a new boss, CEO and team to engage with. Moving to the countryside from London a few years earlier, Olivia wanted to work for an organisation making a difference and making money rather than just the latter. There was a lot at stake working for one of the largest animal charities in the UK and being responsible for their information, data and customer relationship management.

She told me about a meeting she had on the horizon where it was key for her to secure budgets from the board to carry forward the work she'd been promoted to do. We spoke about how to show up at this meeting as her best, most valuable self. We discussed the outfit she'd wear, how she'd prepare beforehand with her Wonder Woman pose, whether she'd sit or stand as she made her presentation and how she wanted to be perceived by the board in three words – *smart, confident, credible*.

As she explained, few people dressed formally in her organisation, but she realised she needed to bolster her authority at the level she was now operating by hardly ever wearing jeans and flat boots anymore and by wearing what she knew suited her and her role – skirts and tapered trousers with low heels.

As a winter palette, Olivia can wear rich, deep, strong colours. So, she embraced her colour palette with dresses, tops and skirts and by wearing strong coloured lipstick. She said that at first it felt as if she was playing a part that it wasn't really her until she had such positive and affirming responses from her colleagues, team, family and friends.

Securing the budgets was easier than she thought, and Olivia's Wonder Woman pose and deep breathing beforehand helped her stay focussed on what she was there to do, rather than be overwhelmed by the perceived pressure of the situation.

I've encouraged so many clients, colleagues, friends and family members to focus on these three things to boost their credibility and confidence – personal colour, style and posture – and even the most cynical have been silenced by results. This is not about downplaying the importance of knowing your stuff. But why would you not want to look *your* best and make the most of yourself when it's so easy and effective? Why would you want to work any harder to convince people you're the professional they can trust who knows her stuff?

SHOULD I STAY OR SHOULD I GO?

'It is confidence in our bodies, minds, and spirits that allows us to keep looking for new adventures'

~ OPRAH WINFREY

The multimillion-dollar question is: 'Should I stay or should I go?' The truth be told – how do any of us ever really know if we're doing the right thing until we've done it and got going enough to find out?

The question I would counter this particular enquiry with is this: "How will you feel if you are where you are in 12 months' time – if things are the same and you're another year older?"

You might respond "You know what, with all I've got going on, actually it will be alright for me. I just need to get more out of what I'm doing." If that's you, then great, I agree.

I'm not an advocate of moving roles, organisations or industries for the sake of it or to prove the point that you can; it's about what feels right for you. It's about you knowing how you feel about what you're doing, how long you can see yourself doing it and your appetite to roll the dice on your career progress.

Think of any big move you've made in your life – getting married, having a child, or buying and selling a home. These decisions were made with the same conscious and sub-conscious influences which you use to decide if or when you'll make a career move.

I look at things through these lenses:

- What will this do for me?

- How do I know if I'm ready and feel right about it?

- What are the benefits of doing this?

- What are the risks and how will I handle them?

- How will this decision affect others?

- Can I see myself being happy with things as they are?

- What would I tell someone else to do if they asked me for advice?

ELLIE S'S STORY

I asked Ellie the question "How will you feel if you're doing what you're doing feeling like this a year from now?" She said in no uncertain terms she probably would have some form of breakdown or blowout. She was so frustrated, feeling her career had stalled and her contributions were going largely unnoticed.

We looked at examples of how she knew this was true for her, who else was involved and what could she try to make things better. Still, she could only see herself leaving. But she wondered how, when and to where particularly since she had become the primary breadwinner.

Ellie will share another part of her story later in the book about how she actually got from this position to one inside another organisation where she 'loves what she's doing' and is on a career succession-planning path only six months into the role. For the moment, her story is relevant in the sense of 'should I stay or should I go?' because she couldn't see how it could get any better.

Trying a few things to re-engage with her boss, team and colleagues, she still felt she was banging her head against a brick wall. So, she started the ball rolling towards her next role with a combination of getting her CV ready to go; learning via the FABB model how to speak about the value of what her experience and skills would do; starting to speak with her network; and actively responding to roles advertised via agencies. She attracted a role that she hadn't even imagined she could. The key was to start looking and activate, not cogitate.

"Call it a clan, call it a network, call it a tribe, call it a family: whatever you call it, whoever you are, you need one."

– ELIZABETH JANE HOWARD

PRINCIPLE 4:

LEVERAGE YOUR CONNECTIONS

It's easy to underestimate the depth and breadth of your network, the team of people you have around you. Start by looking at your current colleagues, ex-colleagues, university and/or school friends, parents' friends, partner's connections, industry connections and social media connections. You'll be amazed at just how many people you are one or maybe two touches away from. Will they help you as you look at your next move or career development? If so, how?

And here's the thing – people in general want to help each other. You know you're normally more than happy to connect people if you're asked and it's done in a certain way.

Some people believe it's too pushy or beyond their reach

to ask for connections and help from others. It's simply not like that at all. In fact, it's more of a case of proceed until apprehended, if you ask me. Assume you can ask for help, and also look for ways you can help too.

We all know people who are only interested in you the day they *need* something from you. My suggestion is to actively be someone who consistently interacts with your network and gets clearer on exactly who they are and what they need. I always say "It isn't about who you know, it's about who knows you" and that's what this Principle is about. Wherever possible, be known and on the radar and then create mutually beneficial and supportive relationships.

WHO KNOWS WHO?

'Great things in business are never done by one person, they're done by a team of people.'

~ STEVE JOBS

One of the best questions to ask when you first meet someone is "How can I best support you?" – not can I or would you like me to, but *how* can I? There's a natural assumption in there that you can support that person and by asking first, you put the first foot forward to build that connection.

You might get a response like "Oh, I'm fine thanks, I don't think you can" and with that you can still say "Well, just know that I'm here and have, like you, a wide network of people at my fingertips. I normally find if I don't know something, someone I know does."

G

With a client looking for a new role, I always ask them about their network, who they know, who knows them, who they know who might know someone, and so forth. That's called leveraging.

Leveraging, as you know, is about making the most of something. As my dictionary states 'to use something to maximum advantage.' You might think to yourself that this is a cynical approach directed towards your network. I don't. I'm not advocating take, take and ask, ask. What I am encouraging you to consider is *who* you can support, help, connect, share information with and, in turn, who you might call upon for the same. As it's been said 'success doesn't happen in a vacuum, it happens with a team'.

In her book *How To Be A Power Connector*, Judy Robinett talks about her three 'golden questions' which help build trust and make your network more robust, sustainable and, let's be honest, interesting for everyone. Her three questions are:

1. How can I help you?

2. What ideas do you have for me?

3. Who else do you know I should talk to?

I like the energy and the intention of these questions. The questions are both two-way and presume you can help, they have an idea for you, and they know someone else. You're not asking the closed question 'Do you know anyone who…?' which often leads to a 'No, can't think of anyone.' You're asking different, more strategic questions which, in the spirit of driving your career bus, will likely steer you towards your next move. People you know will give you ideas, references, introductions and guidance if you consciously build out your network and ask for what you want.

MORE ABOUT ELLIE S

In the previous Principle, we talked about Ellie in 'Should I Stay or Should I Go?'. We learned that she had used her network in a very smart way to find her new role. When I started to work with her on whether she should move on or make her job more sustainable, Ellie asked me if I'd be prepared to travel to her offshore location to speak to a women's network she was part of. I said I'd be delighted and we agreed she'd start the ball rolling.

At the same time, Ellie saw advertised on social media a role in a government organisation. She just *knew* it was for her. The director on the Board of the Women's Development Forum Management Committee also worked for this organisation and was someone Ellie had worked with previously. So, while she nervously and excitedly sent her CV to apply for the role, Ellie arranged coffee with her connection to discuss the future events where I might speak.

I encouraged her to reference that she'd applied for a role where this woman worked. Ellie's connection was excited to hear this. In fact, she said that while it wasn't going to involve her at the early stages, down the line it would. They agreed if she got further in the interview process, they would ensure they didn't compromise their positions. What is so helpful to understand is that the coffee offered something other than asking for career advice. It opened the door for Ellie to discuss the role while showing her ability to bring ideas, connections and contributions to a voluntary organisation they had a mutual interest in.

After a series of interviews, psychometric tests and live case-study experiences, Ellie was offered the job and she now is part of the career succession plan pathway to one day step up into this same connection's role.

I love the circular nature of this story and how Ellie went from frustrated and disempowered to assertive, brave and strategic via the decision to invest in herself and to use her network. As a result of this process and putting herself out there, Ellie was in fact offered two other roles, but she chose carefully based on career progress potential, remuneration and the challenge of what the role offered.

USE YOUR FINGERTIPS AND GIVE

'I've learned that you shouldn't go through life with a catcher's mitt on both hands; you need to be able to throw something back.'

~ MAYA ANGELOU

Who can you help on their way? Who can you offer input,

advice, an idea, a connection or some insight? There's the universal law of giving back when you've received and the reciprocal law of giving in advance of receiving.

One of the quickest ways to boost your network and connections is to closely look and think to yourself "What do I know you're interested in or affected by?" As you look at the names of those you're connected with, I suggest making some form, table, spreadsheet or mind map. With those names in front of you, consider each person through the lens of:

- Where did we meet?

- Who introduced us?

- What made us connect initially?

- What do I know about you?

- What do I think you know about me?

- Who or what could I help you with?

- Who or what could you help me with?

You don't even have to write these responses out. Just asking yourself the questions will prompt you to some insight. Then, go out first and give. Give information or a link to an article you've spotted. Give, by offering to buy a coffee or quick sandwich. Give, by sending a magazine you enjoyed. The phrase 'I saw this and thought of you' has a magical effect. It tells the recipient you thought of them, and you remembered something about them. It also may just prompt a thought, idea or inspiration for you from them.

I can't tell you how often I've heard clients tell me that they attracted opportunities, introductions and invitations just by consciously and consistently connecting, thinking about what people are interested in and looking for ways to help them *first*. You don't have to know where they may lead you, but the key is to attract them and keep opening the windows.

MY STORY

When I first started my coaching practice in 2006, I needed to work with six corporate case studies for at least six individual sessions each and then write up their situations, the coaching methods we used and their progress. I started with my network. I looked at who I knew and who would know people stuck in their careers or at some form of crossroads. I just needed to ask.

Here's the magical part though. I didn't just ask "Do you know anyone who'd like some free coaching?" which is the way many offer this opportunity. As my coaching qualifiers taught us, no one wants coaching. They want the *outcome* of coaching.

So, I asked six close connections "Who do you know who is stuck or at a pivotal point in their career and wants to work out what their best next move is towards promotion or a life change?" Just phrasing the question that way is magical

– *who* do you know, not *do* you know. Then, when you add the outcome of the invitation, it becomes very compelling.

I ended up securing my six cases studies within the same week. From one of the case studies, I was introduced to more than 50 clients and generated a six-figure sum over a three-year period. And that was just *one* of the case studies.

So, with this in mind, what could you offer with a no-return favour that sows a seed at the same time? If you're looking for a new role, your version of my question could sound like this: "Who do you know who might be looking for someone who knows how to get compliant deals signed off by the regulators?" or "Who do you know who could use a legal team with insurance expertise without having to have them on their payroll?"

Then you go silent. If you're speaking to the person, you wait for them to think. If you've emailed, you can say "Let me give you a couple of days to think about it and I'll be in touch again then".

THE POWER OF QUICK REQUESTS

'Sometimes questions are more important than answers.'

~ NANCY MITFORD

The days of pressing send on an email and waiting overnight for the response seem long gone with 'Did you get my email?' being the chaser to the first message after about 30 minutes if you're lucky. Maybe I'm exaggerating a touch, but maybe not? But quite simply people are just very stressed about time and everything seems to be time-sensitive.

That's worth paying attention to since people appreciate and respond more easily to the word 'quick.' Not that you're supposed to be like a spinning top and exhaust people with rapid speech or actions, but what you offer, ask, share or invite can easily include – initially at least – the word quick.

We can find time for a quick coffee, question, chat, catch-up, or lunch meeting in a way we don't so easily for one that isn't. I know this isn't a hard and fast rule and depends on the relationship, but in general, try asking for a quick call or an answer to a *quick* question. Here are a few suggested scenarios and how you might pose your quick request by call, email or face-to-face:

o **To reconnect with a past work colleague**. "Hey Tom, I know it's been a while and so much has developed on your side as well as mine. Can I buy you a quick coffee next week as I'd like to discuss something with you, and I know you'll be able to help?" People love being told they'll be able to help you. They will invariably, so hint about it to them up the front.

o **To find out what opportunities there may be in another organisation**. "Hi Jane, your name came to mind when I was discussing XYZ company. When do you have time for a quick chat about a few interesting developments?" The quick chat involves

developments; she doesn't know if they're yours or

hers or both and yes, you always have developments.

- o **To investigate another industry where a friend works**: "Hey Mike, when would be a good time to buy you a quick lunch about working in the X industry? You know so much and so many people, and it would be good to hear your thoughts."

You can sense in these three *quick* scenarios that your intention is to connect and not to take up too much time. You've given the person enough information about your request but not everything.

As Your Career Success Cycle™ keeps evolving, one of the best investments you can make is in your own network. Sometimes, the best thing you can do if you're feeling a little stuck or stale is to get in touch with someone and arrange a chat. Even if you have no agenda other than to connect, invest that time finding out what's going on with them, what they're struggling with and look at ways you can support them. As with the 'Use Your Fingertips and Give' strategy, being conscious of giving your time while at the same time respecting others' time is crucial.

So, here's a quick question for you – when will you arrange a quick catch-up with someone you know is long overdue?

REBECCA'S STORY

Rebecca and I worked together on getting her ready to move from her company of 23 years following a restructure. Having worked in the same global bank for all this time,

Rebecca told me that she was well-known and had moved regularly over the years. The challenge for her was going outside the organisation where she wasn't so well-known. She had numerous questions. How and where to start? Who to speak to and what to say? How she should come across in writing? How should she handle headhunters and negotiations?

When we started getting Rebecca's CV up to scratch and then mirroring her LinkedIn profile, she told me she was apprehensive but also quite excited. There's nothing like putting yourself outside of your comfort zone to make you dig deep into your experience and identify some of the key skills you want to lead with as you move your career forward.

Things started to take shape quickly and I encouraged Rebecca to start sending out 'quick' emails asking for a coffee or a catch-up lunch with her warm connections. Within six weeks, she'd been approached for a role internally as well as two roles externally with other global banks. Both the external roles came to her as a result of arranging quick catch-ups with her network. She decided to move to one of the external banks after looking at the options and sizing up the scope and scale of the opportunities, the rewards and progression plans offered.

What I find particularly inspiring about Rebecca's story is that she didn't wait or hesitate. She also didn't panic. Knowing she had a certain amount of money to act as a cushion if she did accept the redundancy package enabled her to carefully and calmly consider her options. At one point, there was something of a competition between the two external approaches as to who would attract her.

Without having the experience and wake-up call of being 'let go', Rebecca would never really have known the true value of her experience, let alone her network and the value of the wider perception of the work she did. As a result of this experience, she now knows that if she has or wants to, she can do it again. And again.

FOLLOWING UP AND NEXT MOVES

'Your networking is not working if you fail to follow up. The fortune's in the follow up.'

~ JIM ROHN

There's a state of mind which I believe helps you to follow up more naturally and without the fear of bothering people. Once you've put your feelers out for whatever it is you're looking for, it will require you to be intentional about getting feedback, a response and a next thought. Whatever it is you've asked for or put forward, being passive in these moments is rarely the route I recommend.

I suggest checking in with people rather than checking up. Listen to these statements: "Just checking you got my email" or "We met last Thursday and wanted to check that you've got all you need" or "Did you get a chance to speak to XYZ?" These might be what you *want* to say, but I suggest you follow up with more intention for something to happen in a way which doesn't feel needy or pushy.

Just like most sales-type situations requiring between five and seven touches – meetings, calls, documents and the like – your quest for your next move or your wider opportunities will usually require several touches too. So here are a few pointers for how to follow up – and continue to follow up – in a confident, comfortable and intentional way.

○ **When you leave an interview or meeting**. Ask as you round things up: "So great meeting with you and just so I'm clear, what happens next?" There's a reason for this. You're asking them to commit by saying what happens next. It's more effective than you reeling off a list of understood actions. Ask them and then go quiet. This moment is key for you to hear them commit to what will happen.

○ **Follow up when you've said you will without hesitating**. After an interview, I always recommend that you drop a quick note thanking them for their time. Tell them how you found the experience to be interesting and useful and then, in the spirit of intention, remind them of what you understand will happen next. "And as we discussed, I'll look forward to hearing about developments by next Wednesday or before." It shows you to be both assertive in a polite, clear way and, at the same time, shows you listened.

○ **You followed up and checked in but still haven't heard anything**. Again, you can call or send an email with some other piece of information or a quick question that often prompts a response. If you've seen an article or remembered something you want to add, send it. "When we spoke last week, we discussed *whatever it is* and I remembered I was involved in *example* and have a few lessons to tell. Let's discuss when we meet." You're being vague but adding a hook.

○ **The landscape's changed.** Say you're in an interview process externally or you're being considered for an internal role and you have another approach or your circumstances change. This can be where you hesitate, thinking you don't know what to do or who to tell what to. Stop this spinning and just drop a note or have a quick call to update the person. If you have another approach, then it's pertinent information to share. After your opening preamble, you can say "I've actually been put forward for a role at another organisation and, as I'm still very keen on your role, it will be helpful to understand how things are developing." My point is to be out of the gate first and be positive and intentional about it. Your intention is to show up, respond, be remembered and find out what you want to find out rather than to be passive and wait. Most of the time driving the conversations or responses in this way is preferable to waiting.

Sidebar note: Sometimes, waiting – or 'adopting the art of masterful inactivity' as I've heard it named by a client – is strategic. You can wait with intention, but if you actively want to go for something or build a relationship, put in a little effort and follow up. As John C. Maxwell says: 'Diligent follow-up and follow-through will set you apart from the crowd and communicate excellence.'

"Job interviews are like first dates. Good impressions count. Awkwardness can occur. Outcomes are unpredictable."

– UNKNOWN (BUT SPOT ON –
HAVING HAD A NUMBER OF BOTH)

PRINCIPLE 5:

SHINE IN INTERVIEWS & APPRAISALS

Often, just the very word 'interview' strikes fear into the hearts of otherwise ambitious women. There's a perceived sense of the potential for failure and judgment and for feeling out of your depth or like a rabbit in the headlights.

A more effective and truthful way to approach an interview is to think of it as a two-way conversation. We forget there's the company or person who wants to check us out and understand if or how we're going to be a fit for the role and the organisation. There's also *you* checking out the organisation and the people you meet to ensure *they're* a fit for you and for what you want.

That's how I encourage you to consider the interview process. It's a two-way conversation during which both parties need to shine, reassure and show potential.

You don't want to work for just any old company, nor do you want to jump out of the frying pan of where you are now into the fire of a company that doesn't meet your values or potential. It changes how you approach the interview process when you take on this kind of energy and angle your approach in this way, no matter how much you want the role or want to move. It centres you and makes you more objective. This counts when applying for and going for internal roles just as significantly as it does to applying for external roles.

I always recommend clients treat their interviews like a two-way conversation where they're likely to have a number of questions they want answered too. Not a one-way grilling by the company. That's passive and, in most cases, not doing yourself justice. Sometimes organisations don't encourage you to want further information or to give them a sense of you checking them out. If that's the sense you pick up in the first round of interviews, then pay attention to it. Is that where you want to work if they're treating you this way before you're employed?

PREPARATION & RESEARCH

'Fortune favours the prepared mind.'

~ LOUIS PASTEUR

It goes without saying that before an interview or internal transfer conversation, you'll be looking into what is said about the organisation or team online or by your peers. You'll have read any materials they've sent you and done your own research – and you'll have researched their competition to see who they're up against. You will have accessed LinkedIn, trade magazines and anyone in your network who knows about the company, industry and team. As before in **Principle 2: Discover What's Out There,** remember that research is organised and intentional.

Look up what you can about case studies or the interview process for the company you're going to apply to. You just never know what's already been put out there that will help or give you ideas. The language of the role advertisement, as well as the person you're meeting or have been in touch with, are also worthy of research.

A recruiter once told me she feels encouraged when she notices that candidates have done their research on her and the company that she's putting them forward for. She said it was about them being tenacious and wanting to be prepared, rather than passive and scared.

LINDA'S STORY

Linda had been approached to apply for a role in a major high-street retailer, and it was her first interview in 15 years. She was feeling anxious, concerned she'd be lost for words or out of her depth. Linda and I decided that, despite her being uncertain if the role was really for her, the interview would be part of the training process she needed to land a role she did want.

She had questions about flexible working and hours required at the office because of childcare and her commitment to a youth running club. Both of these points were really important to her and non-negotiable as far as a new role was concerned.

The telephone interview itself was fairly straightforward, and she knew she was more than qualified for the role. However, she got a sense of self-important arrogance from the interviewer, which made Linda's hair on the back of her neck stand up. When it came towards the end of the interview, Linda asked her two questions and was told in no uncertain terms "We expect our senior finance team to be present and visible five days a week to motivate the staff, and we also expect them to be in first and leave last. It's part of our culture." Linda de-selected herself from the process, telling the recruiter that the organisation's expectations didn't fit with her own.

That taught me, and anyone I share this story with, the lesson of asking about what you know you need sooner rather than later. If it's not going to work for you and, if the response was like Linda's with no negotiation and an overarching sense of a lack of trust, find out sooner and don't waste any more of your precious time. The interview itself though was useful. The recruiter respected Linda's approach and carried on looking for other roles for her more purposefully.

This isn't where Linda's story ends, of course. As her search continued, Linda was in discussions about a role that she didn't think she could take. The company wanted her sooner than she was able to move but I always recommend

'Go for the practice'. If someone wants you enough, you'll often find they'll adjust and wait for you.

We discussed the interview conversation, her position, how to play things and the questions the company might ask her. Linda also knew she wanted to have some questions of her own. She had certain things she genuinely wanted answering, and she always liked it when candidates she'd interviewed had the presence of mind and curiosity to ask their own questions.

My advice to her was to 'be brave and objective' and these questions are just that. Linda wants to encourage you to be the same in your interview processes. Here are the key questions Linda used during the process of finding her new role:

- What one word would you say best describes your company culture?

- What key insights would you share with the incoming candidate to make the first six months in the role a success?

- How would you say you do things around here if there's a success or an issue? What is the general approach?

- What do you see as the biggest challenges on the horizon for the company and/or industry?

- What do you see as the biggest opportunities on the horizon for the company and/or industry?

○ If I am appointed, what do you see as something that would be an immediate challenge?

DAWN'S STORY

We heard from Dawn during Principle 3 when she prepared her CV after years in the same organisation. Well, she has another lesson to share with you. When Dawn was in the running for three roles, one of them was particularly interesting to her, and she was about to go for her third interview. This time it was going to involve a case study.

Dawn researched online both the organisation and their interview process, adding 'case studies' into her search. Up came an example of an interview within the organisation and a sample case study. It had been posted online and while it wasn't the exact situation she was given, it helped Dawn to understand the process and prepare more specifically around certain criteria that were mentioned.

I do believe that the response you receive is only as good as the question you ask. If you think about any online search, you need certain specifics to get to where you want to go. Dawn was actually so specific she thought it would be useful to just see what came up and was not expecting to get the golden response from her search. That's the thing about asking. You have to ask because the answer is always 'no' until you do.

BE NIMBLE & FLEXIBLE

'Don't go with the flow. Show them how you roll.'

~ ELSA MENA

When you're invited to go along for a chat or an interview, if you look at your diary and see a commitment, rather than say "No, sorry" straight away, I recommend you buy some time. Try saying "Yes, great, I'd love to come along. I have a commitment at that time. What flexibility is there with the timing?"

You may well be told there isn't any, but by being keen and starting with a positive approach, you may find you get the time you wanted. You can also genuinely say something like "Give me ten minutes to juggle a few things please and I'll come back to you by 10.15 a.m."

It's you being flexible, responsive and crucially, not apologising but sticking to your own commitments too. If you have something that you know is non-negotiable, then say it without apology. "Great, I'm keen to have a meeting too. However, on Wednesday I've got a non-movable commitment. I'm wide open on Tuesday afternoon or all day on Thursday." You don't have to say what the commitment is.

Redirecting to when you *can* speak or meet rather than apologising profusely or feeling like you've only got one shot starts to set the scene for you being someone who has commitments, can be flexible, but who also negotiates. Down the line when we get to the conversations concerning your salary and benefits, we will be looking at exercising your negotiating muscles so let's get them working for you during the interview process too.

When you get to the interview, here are a few key pointers for you:

○ **Take a few copies with you of the CV you sent with your application to hand out if necessary.** Do read it just *before* the interview to you remind yourself exactly what you've written.

○ **Give yourself plenty of time to get there.** Settle yourself with reading your CV and the job specification. Avoid skim reading your emails or any social media distractions. We want you focussed on showing up as your best self without distraction.

○ **Feel comfortable in what you wear**. Take a change of shoes, spare tights, umbrella, water and notepad – the kind of things that are easy to forget but support you and make you comfortable and prepared.

○ **Avoid reading a newspaper or watching the news on any TV** while you wait. They can really distract you from your thought process and can unsettle you. It sounds obvious, but I truly recommend thinking more about what you can do for the organisation, what you know you want to learn, why you want to work for them, what you know you're good at and what makes you special rather than being distracted by what's on the TV.

○ **Have time and space around your interview so**

that you don't have to rush straight there and then rush off again. If you can free yourself before and after a specified interview time, you give yourself the freedom to be there a little longer, have a moment by yourself after the interview to reflect or have a chat with someone to give feedback before you rush off to your next appointment.

SUMMER'S STORY

As part of the interview process for a senior finance role in a small, start-up organisation, Summer was asked if she was free to come for a drink with the team. This was a great sign; it was a spontaneous invitation after a very promising interview.

Having been inside a global bank for more than ten years, it was a big deal for Summer to be out there interviewing to find a fit and promotion. She'd been, as she said, "institutionalised" for such a long time. It was like a breath of fresh air to be among the small team of people and be included in the team drinks.

Because she'd purposefully left herself wide open after the interview, she was able to say yes to the invitation. It was part of the ease of the process, which enabled Summer to say yes to the job offer when it came.

Summer's going to share a lesson as well during **Principle 6: Negotiate More For Yourself,** but for now I encourage you to look for creating space and time around your interviews for who knows what.

PHYSICALLY PREPARING

'Wherever you are, be all there.'

~ *JIM ELLIOT*

It's easy to underestimate the need to be comfortable and present. The word 'present' is the key. By that I mean listening with intention to understand, not just to reply and being able to engage with the person and process and what seems to be required in the moment. It's easy to go through these kind of high-stress situations as if you're in a trance, feeling as if you have to *get through* them rather than actively take part.

There's a huge amount of research around the subject of presence and having presence and being present. My go-to source of materials, stories and evidence is Amy Cuddy who we talked about in Principle 3. When you arrive at your interview or meeting venue, take yourself to the bathroom or a space you find and give yourself two minutes with your Wonder Woman pose to settle yourself.

It's not about being interviewed in the pose, of course. It's about you settling yourself, breathing deeply, reducing your cortisol levels and raising your testosterone levels to enable you to be more focussed, calmer and more *present*. This very act will enable you to make eye contact, think before you respond and ask questions.

MARY'S STORY

Mary had watched the Amy Cuddy TED talk and took on the need to slow herself down and be more present during the interview process. Having been put forward for a role that she ultimately didn't get, she was really conscious during the round of interviews for another role of all the strategies you're reading about here. As an enthusiastic and experienced Irish woman, Mary had a tendency to speak quickly as soon as she was asked something. It was a trait she knew she wanted to change in work-related circumstances.

Each time she was preparing for an interview or a meeting during the process Mary did her Wonder Woman pose. She took time in the bathrooms, in the reception, in a coffee shop nearby, or walking to the meeting to stand straighter, put her shoulders back, focus on her breathing and have her hands firmly on her hips. Each time she did it she knew it made a difference to her delivery and how she was able to ask questions, rather than just respond. She became an active, more equal participant rather than a grateful, slightly breathless candidate.

Despite it being a marathon rather than a sprint process, Mary was appointed to the role she really wanted. She explained a large part of her secret was being more grounded and less anxious. It came down to the physical preparation just as much as the mental.

TECHNOLOGY & INTERVIEWS

'No distractions. Centre yourself. This is your time.'

~ JANE FONDA

It's unusual these days to be interviewed just once or twice. It's more usual to have at least four or more conversations, tests, interviews and meet and greet meetings.

A number of these may be over the telephone or using Skype or video. It's good to be blasé and prepared by just saying "Yes, of course, just let me know the dial-in details" and to expect them, rather than be surprised or put off by them. Teams are global, and you may well be reporting to someone who isn't even on the same continent as you most of the time.

Mastering technology is crucial so start during the interview process as you mean to go on – comfortably and assertively. There's a lot going to be happening for you in moments like these; preparing yourself and how you want to show up is easy and so worth the effort.

Have your notes and notebook close to hand; ensure there is no or minimal background noise; use a good headset if you need one; and clear the background where you'll sit. You don't want your shopping list or, as a client said, her drinks cabinet at home being any form of distraction.

If you have a battery in your doorbell, consider removing it for your interview. Silence your mobile telephone and computer prompts. Remove clunky or jangly jewellery including earrings that may hit your headset. Limit anything that may distract you from what you're there to do and interfere with you being as calm and present as possible.

Ensure you use people's names on these kinds of calls. Ask who's there in the room by saying "Just so I can include them in my thinking" and jot their names down so you don't have to remember.

JENNIFER'S STORY

When my friend Jennifer was interviewed for her first formal, full-time role in nearly 15 years, the first part of the interview – unbeknown to her – was the initial chat she had on the telephone with the recruiter. Jennifer is a friendly, articulate and well-spoken woman, but she was naturally concerned and felt a bit nervous about how she'd come across. So, as is so often the most successful route, she decided to just be herself. She spoke to the recruiter respectfully, but in her normal, friendly way.

This interview was actually her first test since the company was clear that they wanted a person who was comfortable speaking to strangers and able to naturally converse. Having been put through to the actual recruitment process, she only found this out after she was appointed.

The lesson here is *everything* counts. How you respond to questions, how punctual you are, and how you present your CV all count. They're not all dealbreakers, of course, but they speak for and about you when you're not yet in the room.

KEY QUESTIONS & STORIES

'Maybe stories are just data, with a soul.'

~ Brené Brown

Questions, examples, stories and lessons are all part of the interview process to get a feel for who and how you are as a person and how you respond. Some companies have set questions; others are more freestyle.

Depending on who's interviewing you and his or her style, it's best to be ready to respond and, crucially, to give yourself a little pause – just a couple of seconds – before you start. You don't have to pounce on responding; buy a little time by taking a breath, a sip of water, clarifying the question or whatever feels comfortable for you.

You will, of course, know the examples and references on your CV so you can give more details. I can't stress enough the importance of reading your CV through just before each interview or meeting so you can comfortably anticipate what you might be asked to discuss.

So how do you best deliver in these moments? You can take a lesson from Roger Federer, the Swiss tennis champion regarded by many as one of the greatest players of all time. Before he swipes his responding shot, he seems to pause and the ball appears suspended in mid-air for just a fraction of a second.

You can do this too. Take a moment to pause before responding. Choosing your best examples and stories to share requires you to have the presence of mind to think. A great question to ask yourself before you respond is: "What would my best self say to this?" One of my clients shared this as a tip, and it's great to have your awareness of your best self.

Be prepared to expand and not just say "Yes" or "No" if asked closed questions. Offer a little something like "Yes, I do have experience of that."

Interview questions like "What examples do you have about XXX" or "Tell us about a time when" makes it easy to ramble or stumble. Again, **STAR**, which we discussed in How You Speak About Yourself, can guide you to keep yourself succinct, clear and on point.

Learning how to interview is a skill that requires knowledge and practice. There are many excellent books written on this topic. Two that I recommend are: *Why You: 101 Interview Questions You'll Never Fear Again* by James Reed and *Great Answers to Tough Interview Questions* by Martin John Yates

IT'S A MARATHON NOT A SPRINT

'Burning desire to be or to do something
gives us staying power – a reason to
get up every morning or to pick ourselves up
and start again after a disappointment.'

~ MARSHA SINETAR

It's rare that a decision to promote or employ someone happens in just one meeting. You should anticipate having more than one interview and, more likely, many. Like buying a house, it seems like such an easy transaction. You want to move; someone else wants to sell. Simple, right? Except when you start to involve lawyers, vendors, mortgage companies, surveyors, removal firms and a chain of people relying on each other's moves, it gets complicated.

We heard a little about Alison's multi-interview experience on her road to promotion described in Rewards & Your Level of Receiving. Notice I said promotion. Alison's was an internal appointment. Mary, another client had five meetings and interviews before securing her external role. Sonal, another client in the technology field, had five. I have a myriad of other multiple-meeting client examples which prove the premise of treating a career move like a marathon instead of a sprint. For many clients during their interview process, there have been takeover bids or restructures that put recruitment on hold or slow everything down. Expecting it and being comfortable with the potential myriad of meetings allows you to be objective and resilient.

ALISON'S STORY

Alison had a marathon rather than a sprint process to being appointed. As well as different rounds of meetings and virtual interviews on Skype with a team leader in Singapore, there was a major restructure. For a while, the process had to go on hold until the situation and prospects for the role were clear again.

Alison shared that it was her enthusiasm for the role and the potential that kept her going. She'd also been encouraged to go for the role by a number of people when she thought it would be too much of a stretch. It was and it wasn't.

What Alison exemplified is that others can see you're ready before you believe you are and that's something to really pay attention to. Believe them and then make your move towards it. Ironically, it can feel scarier to stay where you are and coast along than to put your name in the game and to rise up to meet potential challenges of the new.

MANAGE RESPONSES & FOLLOW UP

So, you've had your interview or your meeting with a prospective employer or new boss. It's rare that you'll get a decision there and then. Now what? My best advice is to say "Thank you for your time today and what will happen next?"

This is often a moment that gets skimmed over with goodbyes and being seen to the lift or door. Asking this question shows presence of mind and encourages the other person to commit to what will happen. "Well, I'll speak with X and then have a chat with Y and we have two more people to see so we'll let you know by Z what happens next." That's the kind of response you want because after the next point on the timeline, you can send out a check-in request.

Let's also remember you have a choice in this too. It is, after all, a two-way street – securing a new role and being the one secured by the company or team. You too have the power to keep making your own moves. Another company may approach you. You may go for another role and really like the sound of it. You may decide upon reflection not to pursue the role you've been interviewing for. You have your own responses and follow up to consider. It's easy to forget you have your own power to choose in these scenarios.

My suggestion is to drop a quick note to the agency or the person who interviewed you and refer to something specific rather than a bog-standard 'thanks for your time yesterday.' Something specific could be a particular discussion or question you were asked or something which you found surprising or even unsettling. 'It was great meeting with you and X yesterday and I particularly enjoyed our discussion on the challenges of cross-continent working and how to best overcome remote working. I'd like to confirm I'm very interested in the role and look forward to hearing further from you shortly.' You are asserting *your* choice in this moment too.

HANDLING A NO & BOUNCING BACK

'Resilience is knowing that you are the only one who has the power and responsibility to pick yourself up.'

~ MARY HOLLOWAY

No one likes to feel rejected or unwanted but remember that it is a state of mind. Instead of looking at a 'no' as a reflection on you and your skills, look at it as a driver to make you even more determined to look for lessons to learn about what you can do differently next time.

One of my own mentors, Andrea, shared something along the lines of this with me. 'Kay, there's always a lesson and while we can't have a do-over, you can always treat this as training for the next one.'

You never know if the process you went through was a tick-box exercise for the organisation, which means you'd never have been offered the role anyway. Sometimes, interviews have to be held to prove that a protocol has been followed before the appointment can be made of someone who was earmarked for it all along. This is out of your control, but what is in your control is how you respond and bounce back from these perceived knocks.

You may have been unsuitable for the role. Maybe you were considered not ready, too experienced, not experienced enough or just not a fit. You may know some of this, and I always recommend asking for feedback to help you understand and use it for your next move.

Be gracious and assertive. "Thanks so much for letting me know about your decision. While I am disappointed not to be moving forward in the process with you, I would appreciate a little more feedback on your decision and my performance during the interview. This will help me as I move towards another role and also give me things to work on or do differently."

Your version of this is intended to keep you positive and moving forward. I recommend going back with a response no matter what you've been told and however you've been informed. It still continues to speak about you and how you handle yourself in these situations.

Training, preparation, practice and rehearsal – these are always the way to benefit and learn from a pushback and especially one in an interview scenario. There will be a next time and you'll be the better for understanding more rather than be knocked back by it.

Resilience sets people apart. If you are able to bounce back – often after taking time to lick your wounds – you will increase your odds of finding what you want exponentially. Your commitment increases and your energy rises when you keep going rather than assume it was all about you. You won't know the full story necessarily, but you'll know if you want to recommit and use the experience to drive you forward. It is, after all, *always* your move.

ALI W'S STORY

When Ali and I got together to talk about if she was going to dare herself to go for a new role, she was very anxious about the interview process and being able to effectively sell herself. She'd been thinking for some time about moving to a more senior and strategic role within local government. As well as feeling hesitant about putting herself into an interview situation, she had doubts as to whether she could actually do it.

We worked through her skills, looked at what she wanted to do, examined what she thought she could bring to a senior role and discussed how she'd position her skills and experience. It suddenly all became clear.

Her fear of feeling out of her depth was based on not having been through a process like this before. Uncharted waters can feel very choppy but preparation, planning and practice all help you sail more confidently. It certainly did for Ali.

She put herself forward for a role that was being advertised internally. Although she wasn't successful on that occasion, it meant she had come forward and people around her knew she was up for a new role. This led to a better opportunity coming her way soon after which fast-tracked her career in a way the other role wouldn't have.

Once she was in her new role, her confidence soared. She was making presentations when she used to hate standing up in front of people and she came close to being appointed as the senior lead of her team. I say 'close' because when Ali came to my first three-day live event, she joined me on stage to speak of her experience and share with the audience what she'd learned and how daring herself had paid off in so many ways. That wasn't the end of her story at all; it was just the next chapter.

She decided there were certain key elements of her job that she really loved, but the rest she wanted to leave behind. As Ali says, 'It was too hard to be further and further away from doing what I love to do and get bogged down in all the administrative stuff so I had to drive my own career bus out of there.'

With her newfound confidence, Ali resigned, took a leap of faith and started up her own business. We then worked together to get her going with how she talked about what she offered, how she discussed her rates, what her website would say, look and feel like and how her LinkedIn profile would work best for her.

MAXIMISE YOUR ONE-TO-ONES, APPRAISALS & REVIEWS

'Preparation and planning prevents poor performance reviews. You owe it to yourself to know what you've contributed, what you will contribute, and what you want now.'

~ KAY WHITE

No one is ever going to be more interested in your progress, development and potential as you *should* be. While our attention has been primarily focussed on interviewing for outside roles, let's look at the regular internal meetings you have – those ones that really count and are often underestimated.

Your yearly appraisal or year-end review is a key part of Your Career Success Cycle™ because it's a way to gauge how you're doing, how you're being measured and what's on the horizon for you. It's your responsibility to maximise this opportunity and drive the conversations. Let me explain.

I often hear clients say they feel uncomfortable with the spotlight being on them and their developments. You may also feel that your appraisals are a very linear, tick-box exercise that can feel dry and impersonal. It doesn't inspire or excite you, and your boss or person appraising you may be someone you're not comfortable with. Conversely, they may be someone you're too comfortable with so you don't feel you can be really honest and have an objective conversation.

Having the opportunity to discuss and review your year is actually a gift and it's up to you to maximise it. Let's consider three key words, which are the lens I look through with private clients when we discuss how to approach and make the most of their own year-end reviews:

○ **Contribution**

○ **Progress**

○ **Performance**

Using these key words as questions to yourself will help you formulate responses in your appraisals. Your responses to these questions can just be bullet points for you to note and sift through. Some clients take a summary sheet of these lines of personal enquiry into their appraisal with them.

As with your CV, any business-related percentage or monetary amounts you can refer to always adds to the mix. Be prepared to discuss the story and the struggles as well as what you learned and what you overcame.

Your Contribution:
○ Recent: Where have you added value to the company, team, clients and mission of your company? Where have your skills made a difference and what did that mean? What did you make possible?

○ Future: How do you want to align with where the company's going? What do you want to be known for over the next 12 months? What would excite you to be part of? What would you dare to do if you weren't afraid?

Your Progress:

○ In the time since your last review, what are you better at? What have you made happen? What have you started, stopped or introduced and been challenged by? What's changed in the market/team and how have you managed that?

Your Performance

○ Recent: How have you done this? What skills did you draw on? How have you managed yourself? What have you noticed about yourself? What did you have to develop, understand or manage to do that?

○ Future: What do you want to develop? What help can the company give you? What are you prepared to do yourself? (In here, of course, comes the opportunity for future prospects and future pacing yourself and linking both to your earnings.)

As you prepare for your next year-end review, consider why your appraiser should be more interested in you and your progress and potential than you are. You know they're not. That's *your* job.

MELANIE'S STORY

Melanie had just come to the end of the most amazing year in her career. She'd worked flat out as part of a small team to win a piece of business, which was a huge feather in the cap for the company. She knew, as is often the case, that after all the noise died down it would be easy for this win and all that it took to secure this piece of business to be underestimated, downplayed and forgotten.

Using the Contribution, Performance, and Progress questions as her guide, Melanie prepared for her appraisal in a strategic and intentional way, which was something she'd never done before. Her boss literally sat up and listened in a very focussed way. Melanie was easily able to talk through and give examples of contribution, value, progress, skills, challenges, monetary value, prestige and profile. Without her preparation, Melanie said she'd never have felt so clear or assertive.

Melanie gave her boss a summary sheet that highlighted the key points they had discussed and secured her a significant salary increase and bonus. It was a step up for her to behave in this way and paid off not only financially but also as proof of her contribution and sense of worthiness, both key roots in her Expansion Tree – see **Principle 1**.

"If you don't go after what you want, you'll never have it.
If you don't ask, the answer is always no.
If you don't step forward, you're always in the same place."

— NORA ROBERTS

PRINCIPLE 6

NEGOTIATE MORE FOR YOURSELF

You've been offered the role, opportunity or promotion. Do you say yes and go for it? Do you vacillate and wonder whether you can do it? Do you accept the package on offer or negotiate more for yourself? At this moment of power and decision-making, what are you going to do?

Sometimes, women can be in a bit of shock when they are actually offered what they have gone after. All along the process, they may say that they're doing it just for the practice or 'I'll never get it' They're often wrong. So, they are not quite prepared when the offer does come. Let's prepare *you*.

Here's the discussion I often have with clients when they are in a state of fear and excitement after they have been offered a new role or promotion:

"So, you've been offered the role and now you're concerned about what it takes, how to resign, if or how to negotiate and whether you can actually do what's expected of you. Let's say the company calls you and thanks you sincerely for undertaking the process; however, they've actually decided to recruit someone else. *How do you feel if the role is no longer yours for the taking?"*

If your response is "Really disappointed and more than a bit fed up" or words stronger than that, then this indicates a natural sense of caution. Since your response indicates disappointment, you need to acknowledge your fear and, as Susan Jeffers famously said: 'Feel the fear and do it anyway'.

Conversely, if your response is "Actually, really, really relieved," then you must pay attention to this also. If it's true relief, then ask yourself what that's about and if this is the role for you.

KNOW YOUR NUMBER

'Ask for what you want and be prepared to get it'

~ MAYA ANGELOU

Let's assume you know the salary level right from the start of the process. If you're going for a promotion internally, it's often not discussed at the outset as you're already salaried to the company and it's not always seen as important.

Well, it is important – more important than is often appreciated and acknowledged. This is your time to act:

before you've accepted. My suggestion to know your number is to understand what you want your next salary increase to be and to have a firm idea of what you would be really happy with.

It's also about being prepared. I can't tell you how many of my clients have shied away from negotiating their salaries both at the interview stages for a new role and at their annual reviews. Why should anyone else be more interested in what you earn and how it affects your lifestyle and self-respect than you? They're not. That's *your* job.

In these times of women often being the sole, primary, or certainly joint breadwinner, the key is to be comfortable negotiating more for yourself and not waiting to see what's in the offer. By the way, it's also a politically hot time to be talking about your pay levels when companies are being scrutinised and measured about the gender pay gap.

An easy phrase at the outset of negotiations or interest in a role is: "Yes, I'm interested in what you're saying and in being put forward. What's the anticipated salary for this role?" Then pause and wait five to ten seconds to see what comes back. The answer will tell you a lot such as "We have no idea what the salary will be" or "It depends on the candidate's experience."

With that kind of response, you can easily say "I understand, but what sort of range are you thinking?" You may feel squeamish asking this, and that's okay too. If you know or suspect there's a gender pay gap where you are – and sadly it's more often the case than not – seed with 'And knowing we're wanting to keep up with the times around the gender pay gap and equal pay, what is the anticipated salary level for this role?'

This is you naturally and consistently negotiating more for yourself. Don't underestimate or be passive about its importance. This is what pays your mortgage, contributes to your pension, feeds your family and gives you peace of mind. As Barack Obama said: 'Money isn't the only answer but it makes a difference.'

You're a professional woman contributing your precious, finite life energy. Have a number in mind, an amount you want – and I recommend this – a number which makes you catch your breath. You can then have this firmly in your head when and if you are asked about your current remuneration. If you plan in advance, you'll be able to demonstrate why the number you want is justified and why your contribution will be of tangible value to the organisation.

ELLIE S'S STORY

Remember Ellie S from **Principle 3?** She decided to seek a new position and had been through interviews, case studies and role-play. She was excited and just a little bit shocked when she actually received the new offer. However, the salary she had in mind was larger than the salary she was offered.

Ellie decided that come what may, she'd negotiate her salary. This was something she'd never done before. She understood all the benefits, pension contributions and holiday included in the offer but was clear that the role was a big step up for her in scope, scale, responsibility and profile. So when she was offered the role, she took a big breath and negotiated.

We discussed how to actually say the words, which needed to sound strong and positive instead of embarrassed or needy. First she said something like this: "I'm so thrilled to have this opportunity. You know the level I'm earning at the moment and the scale, expectations and profile the role demands. What flexibility is there in increasing my starting salary by X?" I encouraged Ellie, as I do you, to adopt the 'count to 10' strategy. Sit with the tension of the question you've just asked and allow the other person to speak first. Ellie did just this.

After a couple of calls and back and forth discussion, Ellie was offered the role with the inflated starting salary. From the outset, the company wanted her to be fully engaged and excited about the role, and they recognised she was the ideal candidate. Interestingly, they actually acknowledged her assertive stance.

Ellie told me that she was so proud of herself and that she had never negotiated more for herself in the past. It had always been a case of being grateful for what she received rather than having any real input into the process.

RACHEL'S STORY

As a senior partner in a large UK consultancy, Rachel was keen to work at the firm that had been pursuing her. She and her husband discussed the number she would have in mind if and when the time came and it was a number which made her squirm a bit inside. She'd also practiced saying it out loud, something which sounds so rudimentary but is also important so you don't stumble in the moment.

Here's what happened. She was in the final interview and the conversation turned to salary expectations. Rachel had her number in mind but decided to ask the interviewer "Well, I'm interested first to hear what you have in mind for me working for you at this level?" His response was much *higher* than her number.

She accepted their offer and then thought to herself "Why have I underestimated myself?" If she had given her salary expectations first, she would have left money on the table. In truth, there probably was still 'money on the table' as Rachel accepted the offer put first, despite it being higher than her own number. She could have negotiated upwards from the proposed offer. That takes presence of mind and the ability to slow things down in these moments of tension.

It's a classic tactic to be asked for your position first. You know that as a consumer. If someone asks you "How much would you pay for this?" and you say your number, then they're at liberty to let you pay more if you've chosen a number higher than what they would have actually asked you for. Always try to find out where the other party's number is first.

This isn't me encouraging you to be greedy and money-grabbing. Let's be honest, however, these moments are *your* moments. They're worth preparing for and digging in. As the phrase goes: 'Go big or go home'. Until you've agreed and signed the contract, the organisation is in play with you. Remember to be prepared to sit through the tension though and, if it helps, count to 10 while you do.

SUMMER'S STORY

Summer told me in no uncertain terms that before she had accepted her new role she knew she should have negotiated her salary. It was the first time she'd interviewed for a while, and it was an exciting and senior role. It was a 'moment of power', as she referred to it, when the organisation really wants you and you have the power to negotiate. Sharing this with you is to encourage you to use these kinds of *moments of power*.

Once you're in the organisation, the bargaining power shifts but before you've accepted a role, you're equally in play and you'll be sensitive enough to know just how far to dig in before you decide it's a yes or you walk away.

SEED YOUR EXPECTATIONS

'This is a classic negotiation technique. It's a gentle, soft indication of your disapproval and a great way to keep negotiating. Count to 10. By then, the other person usually will start talking and may very well make a higher offer.'

~ BILL COLEMAN

Seeding conversations before asking enables you to drop little ideas and expectations, and clarify assumptions without being direct. Seeding is your natural, strategic and intentional way to get what you want. I describe seeding as 'paving the way for what you want at some time in the future so that when you come out and ask, the pathway is smoother'.

For example, heading towards your appraisal, it's easy to drop a seed a few months in advance that could sound like "Knowing the pay reviews are on the horizon, when it comes to this year I'm sure the 50% increase in my revenue income will be acknowledged in my salary review."

Or during the interview process you can say "The role is sounding exciting and it's going to be one which I know you'll reward well for this level of responsibility."
You can drop seeds at home just as effectively as you can at work. "When we get home and you've tidied your room, let's watch that film you want to see." Can you hear yourself saying that to your child?

When you're negotiating your salary and benefits, seeding is really a way of putting an idea into someone else's head without directly saying it. It starts with knowing salary levels as well as the value you bring.

You have an idea of what colleagues are being paid or you've seen equivalent roles online that give you a sense of the ballpark you're going to be negotiating in. A good website in the United Kingdom is **www.glassdoor.co.uk** where you can research roles, industries and salaries all in a few clicks. As my boss used to say "Kay, information is power."

And make sure that you remind yourself that you're not being paid for the hour you're working; you're being paid for the *value* you bring to the hour. It's the delivery and the results which give the value.

TERESA'S STORY

Teresa heard me speak about negotiating for yourself based on the value you add, not the hours you put in. She had attended my three-day live event in London and fired herself up afterwards to the extent that she had her colours analysed and decided it was time to find a broader, better paid role, and had then been on a round of interviews, secured a new role and was already in post. She'd also secured a hefty salary increase by sticking to her number and negotiating.

So far so great, but there's more that Teresa can teach us. As she got herself settled into the new post and took on all the responsibilities she knew about and many she wasn't expecting, she realised she'd undersold herself. Instead of sulking or confronting, she began seeding during appraisals, one-to-one updates and team meetings.

She seeded about the value-adds she was introducing and what they were accomplishing. She seeded by saying she knew this kind of contribution would be rewarded in the next salary reviews, without waiting for an answer but setting an intention with a seed.

It paid off when the time came. Teresa had a series of meetings signing off her probation period. It was in these meetings that she brought up the subject of the extent to which the scope of her role had widened and the value she was adding. She received a mid-year review and salary increase that was natural and felt comfortable because she hadn't saved all the developments and observations up and delivered them on the same day. Teresa had *seeded* her way there.

DEAL OR NO DEAL?

'You get in life what you have the courage to ask for.'

~ *OPRAH WINFREY*

Just as knowing your number is important, and so is consciously understanding what may make you walk away or take yourself out of the running for a role. I believe it's an energetically strong and important assertion to make that certain things are key for you and, without them, you may well walk away or deselect yourself.

If you know there are dealbreakers, then I encourage you to be clear about them as you go into the process of a move. A few common ones are being able to work from home at times, leaving as often as possible at a certain time to pick your children up from school, being home at night or flying business class because of back issues. These are just a few examples of what can be crucial to you.

As the interview process moves forward, you'll be able to gauge when you should clarify and negotiate, and what you can live with. The key, however, is to have thought about them beforehand.

Also look at options. Rather than the whole salaried amount you want, you could consider bonus payments at an agreed time, staggered payments rather than up-front, extra holidays, working compressed hours, additional pension contributions or more or less of a notice period. These all count and they are all possibly negotiable, but only if you *ask*.

ELSA'S STORY

From the start of the interview process, Elsa had been upfront about the importance for her of working four days a week and having Fridays at home. She'd worked her way up through various organisations to board level, working this way for over 20 years. Sometimes she worked from home on the Friday but generally worked more hours during the four days to make up for the fifth day.

It was, however, a sticking point for the organisation interviewing her. Since they had approached her directly, she felt she had a fair chance of negotiating the terms she wanted. As the process evolved, Elsa sensed she was close to being offered the role and was anxious to start off on the right foot and maintain her working rhythm.

She accepted the position. In the negotiation process she pushed back on the salary, but the organisation could not go any higher. They did offer her a 50 per cent bonus, which was far in excess of her current level. This would take her overall package to the percentage increase she felt excited about and reflected the step up in role, responsibilities and challenges. The sticking point was her working four days per week.

Despite her track record of successfully making this arrangement work, the new organisation felt uncomfortable about agreeing to it. Wouldn't it have been easy for Elsa to roll over at this point? Yes and, again, no. It is a key part of how she has made her commitment to her role and her family work for many years.

So, intense negotiations took place. Elsa agreed she would work five days for the first 90 days and then revisit this arrangement to see how it was working once she was in post and proving herself. This was written into her contract. She also asked for more holiday and a change in title which better reflected her responsibilities. Both of these requests were agreed to because she asked and neither would have been offered otherwise.

You can sense that with her commitment and the understanding she'll have as the full extent of the responsibilities reveal themselves, Elsa will be able to renegotiate based on facts and credibility. At the time of writing this book, Elsa's in post and the outcome of this is still being determined, but I sense she'll get what she wants as she's a true implementer and negotiator.

OLIVIA'S STORY

Olivia had just been offered a role on the executive board of her organisation. It was both an honour for her to be working at this level and another layer for her of work, time and responsibility. As women we tend to say: "Great, that's wonderful news, thank you" and don't assume that there is any additional reward to be negotiated. There normally is and, as is so often the case, we have to come forward and ask.

Here's what Olivia did instead. She responded about how thrilled she was and then said a line I want you to have on the tip of your tongue. In a light but clear voice, with me like Yoda in her head, she asked "And how will that positively impact my salary level?" Then she went quiet. Her boss, who is also a woman, actually praised her for asking; she had no idea as she herself hadn't asked but said she would go and find out.

Before her first executive board meeting, Olivia had confirmation of an uplift in her salary for taking on these extra responsibilities and, as her boss said "for contributing in the way you no doubt will".

HANDLING A NO

'Remember that sometimes not getting what you want is a wonderful stroke of luck.'

~ DALAI LAMA

I believe showing yourself to be a strong negotiator and someone who's prepared to take a view is truly a strength. If you get too fixed, sometimes you can lose the bigger picture of what's on offer. You decide if you must walk away or if you want to proceed with what's on offer but not get all that you want. How do you do that with grace and ease? How do you do it without feeling like you've lost your power and handed it over?

You could be in the situation where you've been offered a role or opportunity that you perceive to be worth an uplift in your salary but after having asked, you receive confirmation that there isn't one on offer. Budgets, salary level rules and these kinds of rebuttals *have* to be taken with a pinch of salt.

Look at the opportunity and what it's worth to you – not to the organisation or your clients. Look at all factors. For example, having extra credibility to put on your CV or resumé can often make it worth doing it anyway.

Of course, it's great to have a yes to your request but, rather than walking away, my suggestion is to ask yourself five key questions and take action based on your responses:

1. What will this opportunity do for my experience and credibility?

2. What sort of things will I learn?

3. How will this add to what I want next or where I want to go?

4. What kinds of people will this expose me to and what might I learn?

5. How will I feel seeing someone else take up this opportunity?

From here, you'll have a better idea of the right response for you. Not for the organisation or your boss, but for you. Only *you* have to know this and justify it to yourself. Everyone else can stay in his or her own business if you decide it's worth doing. By negotiating and asking, you've also set the bar high for future discussions once you've started to prove your worth.

"Sunsets are
proof that
endings can often
be beautiful too."

– Beau Taplin

PRINCIPLE 7:

ACCEPT AND MOVE WITH GRACE AND GRATITUDE

After all the work and commitment you've put into finding and securing a new role, it's time to move on and tell others. This can often feel awkward, disloyal and uncomfortable, but it doesn't have to. It depends how you approach it, how you behave and what you say and do.

The following strategies are well-proven from the myriad of my clients who've found new roles after we've worked on boosting their self-confidence and focussing their ambition again. It's the same if you're moving roles internally or moving outside of your organisation or industry. Being a good leaver is a state of mind first and foremost.

WHEN AND HOW TO RESIGN

*'Try to keep your mind open to possibilities and
your mouth closed on matters that you
don't know about. Limit your 'always' and 'never'.'*

~ AMY POEHLER

It goes without saying that you are fully aware of your contracted requirements of your notice period and what to do when you resign. I would normally recommend you avoid resigning until you've signed the new contract for where you're going. You'll take advice about where you stand in the potential gap between health insurance and life assurance policies, as both are key to you and mustn't be overlooked.

First, know clearly who you'll resign to. I can't tell you how many women have asked me who it should be. It's normally the person who you report to – your immediate boss, designated or assumed. When I resigned, I went to our managing director. My direct report boss had recently changed and it felt congruent to resign to someone I'd worked closely with and who I knew would be directly affected.

If you can, I would do this face-to-face with your letter typed, brief and clear and in an envelope. Of course, now it's often the case that your boss isn't in the same office, country or even continent so you need to work with your particular situation. Again, a personal conversation over the telephone would always be my first move no matter what the time zone, and then as soon as you hang up, follow up with an emailed version of your resignation letter.

When you're moving internally, the protocol will be different as normally your boss will have been involved in the negotiation process of your move. You will, however, often have your team to tell, and I believe the most effective way is to hear from you personally.

SARAH'S STORY

It came as a bolt from the blue. Sarah was about to have her year-end appraisal with her boss. During the past six months, she asked for certain things to happen, to be involved in other opportunities and broaden her experience. As her boss was starting to talk about what he could and hoped to do for her, Sarah handed in her resignation.

Sarah had applied for a role outside the industry in an organisation she perceived as both dynamic and exciting. It was a long shot but using a lot of strategies in this book, Sarah shone during her interviews. She confidently put herself forward and talked about all that she would be able to do for the organisation.

They gave her the opportunity, and now she had to tell her boss that she was leaving. While this wasn't ideal timing, you have to work with what you have. It wouldn't have been fair to allow her boss to go through the process of the appraisal knowing she was going to leave.

Being a good leaver means thinking about the other person's experience of you and what you're doing in these kinds of pivotal moments. That's what made Sarah decide she'd use her appraisal meeting time to resign. It gave them time to have a full discussion – an opportunity to reflect together and, if necessary, have a couple of difficult conversations.

BE GRATEFUL & DON'T BURN YOUR BOATS OR BRIDGES

'Don't burn bridges. The person you throw under the bus today could be driving it tomorrow.'

~ GLENN SHEPARD

Whatever your reason for moving on, there's always something to be grateful and gracious about. Even if you're leaving because you can't stand another moment longer with your team or doing what you're doing, you can still be objective as you leave. You will have learned so many lessons and been exposed to all sorts of people and experiences – even if it's that you *never* want to do that again.

In my own corporate role, I lost track of how many people left to go to the competition, full of anticipation for the new and, at times, sharing sarcasm about the old. Then, the situation changes. The company you leave buys or merges with the company you went to. The boss you left to get away from joins your new company. The team you didn't want to work with any more are brought in. Like magic, here you are again. I've seen all these things happen and remember how uncomfortable they were for those who had burnt their bridges.

My suggestion is to do your absolute best to look for the positives in what you've experienced where you were and be objective as you leave. When you're talking about what you're going to do and why, remember you never know where you'll meet again and when or if you'll need the connection. That's strategic as well as energetically strong.

MY STORY

Starting as a secretary and then becoming a personal assistant, I worked for four years at the same company straight from college. I tried to negotiate a pay increase with my boss, and while he was personally supportive, he was unable to secure agreement for what I wanted. I'd just bought a flat and was finding it a stretch to make ends meet so I resigned and found another secretarial role paying what I needed. When I resigned, my boss, Ted, understood although he was very disappointed.

We remained in touch and had lunch together every few months. He'd replaced me with someone who wasn't really a fit for the role or for him. I'd started my new position as a PA at an international recruitment headhunter with great enthusiasm, but soon found I was working in a hotbed of gossip and backstabbing which I just wasn't used to. I learned so much, though, about how to navigate these kinds of conversations without being sucked into them.

After 18 months, Ted and I decided to give working

together again another try. He'd secured the salary level he knew I wanted now and I knew that with the extra experience and confidence I'd gained, I would be much better equipped to take on more responsibility.

At first, it was a bit strange being there again, but I didn't feel I was going back as much as moving forward. While I only stayed for another four years, I motored ahead with building connections and confidence, as well as having great working conditions and more income. That's when I moved into the broking side and, where over the next 14 years, I got to exercise my negotiating and dealing-with-tricky-characters muscles even more.

Then I decided to start my own business and make another move. Even then, the boss I resigned to offered me the opportunity to return after six months. I didn't, but it was a great opportunity to have in my mind. I didn't burn my bridges; we've kept in touch. Most of my colleagues have moved from there to other broking houses, and we are bumping into each other along the way. Some have become clients, which is a whole other story.

HOW TO NEGOTIATE YOUR OUT

'Place a higher priority on discovering what a win looks like for the other person.'

~ HARVEY ROBBINS

Often, you'll have a notice period of between one and six months. In all cases, you can look at negotiating your leaving date. The answer may not be what you want, but it's always worth trying to make it work for all concerned. I always encourage clients to have worked out a few things important to negotiations *in advance* of actually resigning by considering the following:

o What are you active with at the moment, and who's your natural hand-over person?

o What does your boss and his or her boss have going on which you directly feed into, and how will you handle that?

o What things that only you can do must you tie up or sort out before you leave?

o What are you working on which definitely needs your input, but which someone else can start taking over straightaway?

o What timeline would you aim for, and what's the actual date you want to suggest?

o How many working days does that add up to so you can actually say the number rather than approximate them?

Based on these questions, can you sense how much easier it will be for you to negotiate what you want if you resign with a real handle on what's going on with your work and responsibilities? You may even have in mind the person to take over your post. These are all pertinent negotiation tools that come into play as you negotiate your leaving date and reassure your current team, boss and organisation.

Keep in mind, however, that depending on where you're going to, you may find you leave the same day you resign. If you're going to a competitor or an organisation perceived as a threat, you can be asked to leave immediately. I've seen it happen many times during my own corporate career, and it happened to many of my clients and my husband.

JANET'S STORY

Janet had gone for a promotion inside her organisation and was thrilled to have been appointed out of the final ten candidates. The new position involved moving from one part of the business to another with the same effect as a resignation but without leaving the company.

This caused a challenge for Janet since her current boss didn't want to let her go a moment before he had to, and her new boss wanted to immediately begin to include her in business decisions and strategies. While very exciting, it was creating all kinds of stressful push-pull moments for her.

After wondering whether her current boss was in denial about her leaving, Janet had to take a stand and, with my support and guidance, she picked a date. She met with her boss after looking at her notice period, the expectations of the new role and what she had going on. She was no longer waiting for him to get a grip on things. Her action had two very quick results.

By planning for the date and looking at what was achievable, possible and necessary to complete, Janet had a clear plan to reassure her boss in a challenging but determined way. Because her boss felt more comfortable and in control, he then started to implement what was necessary to cover her work.

She started speaking in working days along the lines of "OK, so we've got ten working days before I hand this over, what's the best way to do this?" or "So as I've only got five more working days here, my suggestion is this." There's nothing like painting a stark and real picture about a timeline and how short it is in actual days to focus the mind.

If you say a couple of weeks or a month, it's much more spacious than the truthful 'ten working days' or "I'm here for twenty more working days." What was possible and the scarcity of time became Janet's carrot and her stick to use at the same time.

WHAT TO SAY TO OTHERS

'We all live with the objective of being happy; our lives are all different yet the same.'

~ ANNE FRANK

Often the concern of what to say to everyone can really throw women into a spin. One thing I do know is that the tectonic plates of your normal working day do shift beneath you the day you resign or announce you're moving on. This is something to expect, prepare for and, on some level, welcome.

People's reactions can vary depending on your relationship and their openness. I encourage you to be graceful, grateful *and* assertive as you leave. This isn't a time to be apologetic or fret unduly about what will happen without you. It's a time for you to look forward and to assume the best of your colleagues and company and how they'll react and respond.

Even if some people's reactions show up as envy, it's most definitely not your problem but something to be conscious of and half-expect. People don't always want the best for us – even if they're not fully aware of this – and often our strong decisions make them question their own positions. That's okay; it's not about you. It's their path to walk and their decision to make.

You may find that you quickly feel like a spare part as you are counted out of discussions you'd normally be involved in. That has to be all right with you. You're leaving and, as a result, you're a short-term consideration in the long-term direction of the business. I want you to be prepared for it so you don't get thrown when it happens. Many women are long-term in service where they are and this sense of suddenly being an outsider can come as a bit of a shock.

I sensed this the day after I resigned. I wasn't invited to a meeting about an account I'd normally have been involved in because six months down the line, I wasn't going to be there. It took some getting used to, but it's part of the ride of taking the steering wheel and driving your career in another direction.

My suggestion is always to be as objective as possible.

In the same way I suggested earlier to avoid burning your bridges, being objective enables you to keep yourself clear of too many opinions and story spinners.

Rather than feeling guilty – we as women are experts at that and it's something which I really recommend paying attention to – instead feel very good that you've made a decision and stand behind it. An opportunity has come your way and you've decided to take it. The time felt right and you're excited at the challenge this offers you.

Even if you're making a sideways move, it's still about your choices, lifestyle and objectives. It is not about everyone else's. Here are a couple of helpful, honest and objective phrases for both the promotion opportunity and the sideways or lifestyle moves. The italics reflect my thinking for you, and you can sense how open, objective and decisive you are without guilt or a hint of 'I'm sorry to leave you in the lurch', which is unhelpful for them and disempowering for you.

Promotion Opportunity: 'It was a tough decision to decide to leave and I thought carefully about it. I know you'll be pleased for me (*they won't always but we don't have to worry about that and we can assume they will be*) and it's a great opportunity. I've learned so much from being here (*good, bad, indifferent – you will always have learned so it's easy to say this*) and I'm excited to step up in this way. Thank you for all you've contributed so far.'

Sideways or Lifestyle Move: 'I'm excited to make this move at this time. It's been an amazing learning curve and I know I'm ready for a change. The opportunity to do this makes sense now so I know you'll be happy for me. (*Again, they may or may not be but let's always give them the benefit of the doubt and assume the best.*)'

ELLIE S'S STORY

It was a bit of an anti-climax when Ellie resigned after months of interviewing with outside organisations and trying to work out if there was a way she could stay by making things better. Her boss was based abroad and not available to speak with so she couldn't have a face-to-face with him for a while. Her matrix manager was available so she met with him to chat through the resignation and asked about next steps. It was suggested that a formal letter of resignation be emailed to them both and HR. So, Ellie resigned by a clearly stated, objective and well-crafted email. Then there was silence. It took surprisingly long for her to hear anything officially.

And the response told her what she already knew – she wasn't valued, appreciated, recognised or rewarded enough where she was. Her decision to leave was the right one. Time would tell whether the new organisation was a fit, but it was most definitely the time to go.

Eventually her team got to hear the news, and she handled her exit with grace and gratitude. She didn't make any snide comments or say anything negative about how she'd been treated. This was a smart move as she often comes across ex-colleagues since she's still in the same industry, just working for the regulators rather than the bank.

IF (OR HOW) TO BE HONEST WITH THE TOUGH STUFF

'I can be changed by what happens to me.
But I refuse to be reduced by it.'

~ *MAYA ANGELOU*

It's an interesting dilemma if you're leaving and part of your decision to go is because you've had a negative experience. Do you come clean about what happened and how it contributed to your decision, naming names if needs be? Do you just stay with the non-contentious feedback about a new opportunity being too tempting? Whose interests are you serving depending on your decision? You'll often be invited to have an exit interview of some form and my advice would always be to be objective. Ask yourself these questions:

o What do I actually want to get across in the interview?

o What part did I play in what happened and how will I take responsibility for that?

o Who and what do I know must be mentioned to make this feedback useful and truthful?

o How do I want my feedback to influence the business, team and organisation going forward?

○ If I were to advise someone on doing this, what would I tell him or her?

Make sure you take notes if you decide to explain what happened, how you were treated, where you felt something negative could have been avoided and the myriad of other incidents that led to your decision to leave. Keep yourself on point and be specific with examples. It helps the other person understand and gives them something tangible to work with. It's part of your legacy of being a good leaver to give this kind of feedback, if you believe it will avoid such a situation for someone else in the future.

HOW TO KEEP IN TOUCH

'Life is like riding a bicycle. To keep your balance you must keep moving forwards.'

~ ALBERT EINSTEIN

At this point in your life, you know that your friendships have cycles as does everything. Friends who were so close at one stage in your life at school, university, sports clubs and workplaces shift and change as all our lives shift and change. We have, as one of my own friends said "Friends for a reason. Friends for a season. Friends for life."

Trust me, these shifts happen even if you're moving floors at work. I've experienced the difference when you don't have the same level of contact you did before. Accepting it, expecting it and moving forward is all part of the ride to new pastures where you will attract new people into your life and let go of others.

My point of including this in the book isn't about sharing with you how to keep true friends. That's something you're no doubt already adept at doing. It's more about allowing yourself to let go of certain people without any guilt or sadness and recognising that the common thread you had has shifted. It's also about separating friendships and connections. They're not the same and aren't supposed to be.

You only have to think of the people you're working with now; even though you might be really close, once you change direction or they do, the relationship naturally shifts. It's all good. It's part of making your own purposeful progress in the career direction that suits *you*.

MY STORY

As part of a team of around 50 people, I had a lot of really good connections and friends in the office. A lot of us had been there more than five years and grown up together in a way. Late evenings, drinks after work, weekend working, business trips, client lunches and dinners as well as the day-to-day discussions all created connections – some of them very strong.

When I look back, I realise that it was probably the freest and most fun-loving time in my life and career. I don't think I've ever laughed as much as I did at times in our office. I also recognise there were times when I truly felt I'd explode with frustration, expletives and exhaustion. It was a *season* in my life.

When I resigned, I knew there were about three people I'd stay closely in touch with. As an introvert with extrovert tendencies, that was all I really wanted too. Fifteen years later, I still have lunch with other colleagues, bump into them in the street and find each other on LinkedIn. Some have actually turned into clients as they got stuck in their own careers.

Here's an interesting sidebar. When I look back, I see a pattern that was emerging back then and plays out in what I do now. Colleagues, especially male, used to come and sit in 'Kay's Corner', as it was known. My natural curiosity and ease with going deep into conversations – I'm not fussed about or particularly good at small talk – meant I would know a lot about colleagues and their relationships, ambitions and frustrations. It was a sure precursor to what I do now.

In general, if you look closely at who you're really fond of and connected to, then it's easy to assume you'll stay in touch. In the spirit of knowing you're in a cycle, pay attention also to others who you might just send a note to, get in touch with on LinkedIn or pop by for a coffee. It goes all the way back to **Principle 4: Leverage Your Connections** and is very much a key part of *Your Career Success Cycle*™.

"If you don't design your own life plan, chances are you'll fall into someone else's plan. And guess what they have planned for you? Not much."

– JIM ROHN

PRINCIPLE 8:

NAVIGATE THE FIRST 100 DAYS & BEYOND SUCCESS ROUTE

There's an energy about someone who takes the initiative, rather than just asking about the plans already in place. My suggestion is to take the reins and make your own First 100 Days Plan. It shows you to be someone who wants to hit the ground running and who has taken time and energy to think about how to best be opertional and of value as soon as you start. By doing this, your future boss or team leader will also be more focussed on your behalf.

I can't tell you how often this catches my clients' new organisations off guard, not in a way that has ever backfired but more in the way of them being receptive, respectful and appreciative (if a little surprised). It can make things happen for you in advance of your starting date that otherwise could distract you or slow you down once you do start.

Remember 100 days is just over three calendar months and your probation period is often 90 days. Let me share with you the experiences of many clients who worked on having such a plan in place or in progress before they started and the difference it made.

TAKE GUIDANCE AND USE A PLAN TO GUIDE YOU

'It takes as much energy to wish as it does to plan.'

~ ELEANOR ROOSEVELT

Leading up to starting a new role is often stressful. There's the way you leave where you are as discussed in **Principle 7** and then there's the planning and anticipation for a successful start where you're going. Having a First 100 Days Plan in place to set you off in the right direction enables you to maximise your energy and focus at this key time.

Your learning curve in a new role or organisation is steep and continuous at first. Even if you are taking a similar role to one you've had in another organisation, there are so many things to find out and understand, people to meet and know about and cultural changes to navigate. It's easy to underestimate this and find yourself exhausted. Even with the plan in place, it won't all go as planned. At least you have a 'North Star' – a place to come back to for reference.

When you accept the role and finalise starting dates and

salary, this is the time to say something like "To ensure that I'm up to speed as quickly as possible, I want to put a First 100 Days Plan in place with your guidance and support." While you may not immediately get a firm response, persist. It's so worth it because it makes many things happen which otherwise wouldn't.

JANET'S STORY

Even though Janet was making an internal move in her organisation, it was to a very different role with more responsibility and profile. She was keen to start on the right foot. We worked together to get her ready to be ready, and it was so interesting to hear what happened when she sat down with her future boss to discuss her First 100 Days Plan.

It caught him off guard and made him jump to sorting out all sorts of meetings and discussions that she needed to have and people who needed to meet her. These were all planned in advance of her start date. The key was including him in the plan and asking who else needed to be involved.

A First 100 Days Plan isn't something you do in a vacuum by yourself. It's something to include your new colleagues in, and it becomes one of your first collaborative, strategic moves.

Here are examples of some tasks identified for just the first 20 days to get you going:

○ Meet all stakeholders and hear about challenges and opportunities.

○ Understand priorities – both yours and your stakeholders' and the wider team you're part of.

○ Listen to what's working and what's not working.

○ Hear different perspectives and stay open.

○ Identify key insights.

○ Request weekly updates with key stakeholders and/or your boss to ensure that expectations and objectives stay on track.

For each of these tasks you need to determine when ideally it will happen, who is who, how you meet them and how to gather what you need to know. This is what your stakeholder can support you with.

In Janet's case it meant she and her future boss were very quickly and efficiently working together. He was impressed by her tenacity and the assumption that this was something she would have in place as much as possible before she started.

UNDERSTAND WHO'S WHO QUICKLY

'Everyone has an invisible sign hanging from their neck saying 'Make Me Feel Important'. Never forget this when working with people.

~ MARY KAY ASH

Your first few encounters require you to be truly present to what's going on for the other person, not just for you. This makes you more comfortable and able to recognise where the focus is in these early encounters. If you make the focus on the other person, it frees you to listen, question and be open to what you might be learning.

Often the temptation is to feel you have to impress with your experience, be funny or be something you actually don't feel, instead of allowing yourself to be friendly, curious and open.

Here are a few key pointers of how to 'be' to help you avoid getting overwhelmed and be present enough to enjoy meeting the myriad of people you will likely need to meet.

Be friendly. Shake hands, use your full name and be sure you've heard and pronounced their name correctly. If they ask you why you left where you were or why you've joined their organisation, be ready with your phrases from 'What To Say About It All Around You'. Don't give too much detail or spend too much time on you. Turn the attention back to them. You want to find out about *them* rather than the other way around in these early conversations.

Be curious. Curious is different from nosy or demanding. Curiosity's about having a genuine interest in understanding more. Ask lots of open questions – not like a quizmaster – but with that curious energy of seeking to understand. 'How long have you worked here and what brought you to the industry?' 'What are the main challenges you're experiencing at the moment?' 'Where do you see opportunities for the business in the near future?' These kinds of enquiry questions encourage the other person to speak and show that you're interested in them, rather than in babbling about yourself, which can easily happen with a little anxiety seeping out.

Be open. Early encounters are more about connection, knowing others and being known, than fully understanding or thinking you understand too much. Time will tell you more about what you need to know. That person who was offhand, disinterested or really excited to meet you doesn't necessarily show you who they really are. They're showing you themselves at a moment in time and have other things going on competing for their attention. It's easy to judge in these early encounters and, of course, easy to be judged yourself. The more open you can be, the more you learn. The more you learn, the more you have to draw upon as you get going.

MY STORY

When I moved divisions within the insurance broking house, I had a very quick circuit of introductions. I met someone called Jan who had, as she told me afterwards, a wariness about me as I seemed too at ease too quickly as I knew so many of the team already. Apparently, I came across to her in a way that she didn't initially trust so she decided we probably wouldn't get on together and I could sense this. Initially, I didn't let it concern me too much, but it gave me a bit of a jolt when I found out she was going to be one of my mentors in my new role. It would have been easy to not have much else to do with her, judging from that first encounter. But, that's not how it worked out – fortunately.

Neither Jan nor I showed our true selves in that first encounter. As one of only a handful of women brokers, Jan became one of my closest friends and allies. We remain friends all these years later. If we had based our relationship only on that first introduction, we would have missed out on so much fun, success and mutual learning.

ELSA'S STORY

Elsa, a natural extrovert and great communicator, made it part of her First 100 Days Plan to meet, greet, listen and learn from as many people as possible, especially key stakeholders.

She was in the post room and went over to a man with her hand outstretched. She warmly introduced herself and explained briefly about her new role and how keen she was to get going. She then asked him about what he did, and he told her he was an external motorcycle courier who'd just delivered a parcel. He didn't work there at all, but – as surprised as he was – he wished her well all the same.

I love this little aside because it shows the depth of how much Elsa cared as she went about implementing her plan. It was Elsa who first told me about how she'd worked a First 100-Days Plan when she started her new role and shared her experience of doing so with one of my private mentoring groups, inspiring a number of them to do the same.

What I want you to take from this is that a goal without a plan is just a wish, as it's said. It's the plan – the how you'll do it – which sets you up for success. While you are likely to go off track at times, you have the plan to measure yourself and discuss with stakeholders as you go through your key probation period.

JOIN IN AND BE ON THE RADAR

'Courage starts with showing up and letting ourselves be seen.'

~ BRENÉ BROWN

As you take your place on your team and begin to understand your new role, the pull on your time and attention can be overwhelming. That's why it's important to pick wisely where and how you show up.

It's important to look for opportunities to be on the radar in your new place. Clearly, I don't mean to be at any and every meeting and every after-hours drink gathering but do pay attention to being at *some*. It's about accelerating the process of being known and being seen by others.

Look for opportunities to join committees, networks or steering groups so you can meet more people and contribute. This form of contribution is different from your overall role and is another form of stretching yourself to see who's who in the zoo and how things get done where you are.

Within your first 100 days, I recommend you attend at least five different social events and put yourself forward for a maximum of two or three committees or steering groups. You may not be accepted for them, but the very gesture of offering says something about you. Your stakeholder or boss is often the first port of call for this offer, but don't do it in a vacuum either. Offer yourself more widely so you are known by more people as someone who's prepared to contribute without being asked.

As with all things, balance this with a healthy "Ah, I'm fully committed at the moment but thank you for thinking of me. Can I come back to you another time if there's still an opportunity?" If you feel you're being taken for granted or have enough for the time being, don't slam the door; just push it a little closed for now.

SONAL'S STORY

For Sonal, joining a new company within a new industry meant that *everything and everyone* was new. One of the things she saw as both strategic and in line with her personal values was to offer to contribute to the internal women's network group. Putting herself on the radar with other senior women meant she quickly got to know and became known to many more people than she would otherwise have been.

She involved herself in arranging and supporting internal events and found many useful connections this way. These kinds of networks and groups attract senior support, and it's a smart way to make yourself more widely known in your early days in an organisation.

It's smart at any time, but as you start somewhere, it's

particularly key. You are a learning machine at first, noticing everything and not taking anyone or anything for granted. Notice what you notice in these early days; it's all building up a picture for you.

You might think you don't have time to offer any more of yourself as you start a new role, but this is one of the best investments of your time. It also means you get the benefit of different perspectives in your organisation, the potential of other mentors and, of course, friends who've gathered around another common objective.

FOCUS ON A QUICK WIN DELIVERABLE

'Success is built sequentially. It's one thing at a time.'

~ GARY W KELLER

As part of your First 100 Days Plan, try to identify what would constitute a quick and impactful deliverable for your new role. Ask your colleagues and stakeholders "What would be the best use of my time for you at this time?" or "How can I make the most difference knowing what's challenging us at the moment?"

It's important for your own confidence and for those around you to see you implementing and getting yourself quickly up to speed without drowning in the detail. It's a balancing act, but it does work when you look at what you're there to do, what's going on and what's on the horizon. Then, invite input as to where you can make the most difference.

You may be crystal clear already or it may have been part of your interview and contract-signing stage where you'd focus on a certain area as soon as you start. More often than not, however, it's not clear when people start where they would be most effective. That's for you to find out, investigate and identify. Crafting your First 100 Days Plan in collaboration with your new boss will help you with this and it can be part of your ongoing conversation.

JEANETTE'S STORY

It had been a rough ride for Jeanette. Having worked at the same organisation for just over 30 years, she'd risen to a senior level and experienced takeovers, mergers, restructures, and a myriad of different management structures. Her roles had shape-shifted to such an extent that she found herself feeling on the periphery of things, not fully contributing or satisfied. Jeanette had been through a period of feeling lost, undervalued and truly stuck. She wanted to be part of a dynamic team, but it had eluded her. She was at the point of looking outside the organisation.

Jeanette was experiencing an important pivot point we all need to pay attention to. If you wait too long or expect things to change without taking action, you can find your own self-esteem and confidence taking a severe dip. This then makes you question your worthiness and ability to show up and shine in an interview.

As one of my close mentoring clients, this was something we discussed. I encouraged Jeanette to ensure her CV and LinkedIn profile were both up to date and to get in touch with her network to start the process described in **Principle 4: Leverage Your Connections.**

Then it happened. An opportunity opened up where she was, and one of her connections pointed her in the direction of it. A team of traders was in desperate need of support to implement a new strategy to enable them to be more commercial and effective, and remain on the right side of the regulators. They needed someone with a special set of skills who understood the business and had a commercial head; understood people and their different styles; and knew how to introduce structure where there was little to none.

The essence of the role was enabling successful traders to keep trading and to do it in parallel with the needs of both internal and external clients and the regulators. It was Jeanette's moment, and she didn't hesitate.

When she first agreed to take on the role, it was on a trial basis both ways. What's key is that Jeanette didn't tiptoe around the issues the team were facing. She dived straight in and asked hard, confronting questions, contributed to tough decisions and quickly demonstrated her skills at creating structure. It became 'a no brainer' that she'd be offered a permanent post. In her new role Jeanette is herself transformed in confidence, vitality and energy. She's needed, respected and relied upon.

The lesson I've taken from this evolution in Jeanette's career path is that it's not over until it's over. Opportunities do arise, and you need to prepare to rise up and meet them quickly –

not by fretting and wondering if you can do it – but just saying yes and then going for it. Jeanette's story reminds me of a quote from Seneca, the ancient Roman philosopher: 'Luck is what happens when preparation meets opportunity.'

MANAGE BEING MANAGED

'What gets measured gets managed.'

~ Peter Drucker

It bears repeating once again that no one will be *more* interested in your career development or direction than you. When you start out in a new role, you will be competing for attention with a myriad of other day-to-day responsibilities that your boss or stakeholder has. You'll also likely find that when things were supposed to happen, they don't.

The induction course you were promised may be put back or the weekly one-to-ones you wanted may slip to fortnightly or monthly. Your invitations for attendance at key meetings may be overlooked. Recruitment of certain team members may fall off the agenda. This is why I want to encourage you to continue to drive your own bus and steer things the way you want them to go as far as possible during your early days.

Throughout this book, I've reiterated the responsibility we have to make what we want and need important. We cannot wait for or expect others to always do what they say they will do. Things slip, but let's be clear about not allowing one of those things that slips to be you and what you need.

This again comes back to your self-confidence, expectations and how you put these across. Mark a date in the diary to discuss something you want rather than waiting for the invitation. Remind people of what was said in a light but intentional way without apologising, along the lines of "I understand there's a lot going on. The weekly one-to-ones we schedule really keep me on track as I get going."

The premise of managing being managed is one of the key responsibilities you'll always have. Sheryl Sandberg said in her book *Lean In* that 'the most important career choice you'll make is who you marry' citing the importance of sharing personal responsibilities, receiving and giving support.

This is true of your boss and whoever else manages you. They play a huge role in your success and how well you're known, rewarded, put forward and encouraged. They can easily – either intentionally or accidentally – slow you down and keep you back.

Always look at ways to manage *how* you're being managed from the first day in your new role. It's not necessarily fair, but it's absolutely true that no one is more interested than you *should* be on how you're progressing and what's happening next for you. That's why getting in front of people, discussing your plans and objectives and understanding how they're being received, reviewed and valued is *your* job – no one else's.

If anything, I think this premise is freeing and puts you in the driver's seat again. This premise applies throughout your entire career, whether you're conscious of it or not.

ANN'S STORY

After working for more than 14 years in an organisation, things changed rapidly with a restructure, and it was time for Ann to move on. It was an emotional rollercoaster for her to make the decision to leave the organisation after such a length of time and at such a pivotal point in her career. She'd been promoted twice in a short space of time, was respected by the management and was really appreciated by her peers and team. The writing was on the wall, however, and she didn't like the direction the company was going in.

With a network of connections in her industry, it wasn't long before Ann found another role that seemed to be a fit for her. She was excited and, at the same time, anxious about how the change would work.

After six months, it became clear to Ann that she wasn't a fit for this new organisation. Things took so long to happen, and her boss was indecisive and somewhat in awe of Ann's can-do attitude. Without hesitating for long, Ann drove her bus out of that organisation and into another one. An ex-colleague had approached her to join her in a senior role in another firm in the same industry.

As Ann shared, the hardest move in this series of career changes was the first one. After making that first leap, the subsequent move was easier. Here's the extra layer to Ann's story. This new role didn't work for Ann either. There was another restructure and suddenly it was time to find another role.

What Ann taught me is that if you believe you have skills and experience to offer and can pick yourself up after a setback, you'll always find your way to your next role. By working with her networks, following up with prior colleagues and managing her own path rather than waiting to see if it got better, Ann has negotiated her way to another organisation which feels more of a fit.

HAVE YOUR OWN ANNUAL REVIEW

'Both happiness and unhappiness depend on perception'

~ Marcus Aurelius

I have already given you some guidance to help you shine during your annual appraisal. But what about your own, personal how-am-I doing annual review? Each year I take time, just before the end of the year, to review the year gone by. I do this with my client groups too, encouraging them to examine the lessons, developments and messages from the year coming to a close.

You'll be amazed what you learn about when you review just how much has happened during the year and consider your perception of the developments and how they have affected you. It's a moment to examine where you are now with your plans, hopes, goals, dreams, issues and challenges. It's also just a moment in your time – no one else's – and each year you, like the landscape around you, change.

Most people skip from one year to the next with a vague idea or wish of what they want to make happen, but not a clear plan. We also tend to generalise about what the year just gone has been about. There will have been so many highs and lows, lessons and messages for you, if you take time to find them out.

Having created a handy Your Year End Review & Planning Guide, I've combined questions to guide you to review the year and start to plan for the year ahead – not just work-related but also on personal, health, well-being and relationships.

It's a gift to give yourself, and I only wish I had learned to do this earlier in my own career path. We invest time and energy in going through the process in our professional lives, which effectively ticks certain boxes for your organisation, but we don't, as a matter of course, do this for ourselves.

If you want to try this, each year I upload an updated version of my guide and you can download a copy for yourself at: **www. kaywhite.com/bookresources.**

What comes out of this exercise may well inspire you to take your next step in your own personal career success cycle either where you're working now or where you want to head towards next.

It is, after all, *always* your move. Now you know why and most importantly, what to do for this next move and, of course, *all* the moves you make after that.

"The truth is you don't know what's going to happen tomorrow. Life is a crazy ride and nothing is guaranteed."

– EMINEM

AT *ANY* GIVEN POINT IN YOUR CAREER SUCCESS CYCLE

This book wouldn't be the torch to guide you without this section. It's not a Principle by itself. Rather, it is a *permanent zone of possibility* around all the *8 Principles of Your Career Success Cycle*™. To omit it would have been to short-change you, the reader and strategic career woman you now are.

Having had ovarian cancer when I was 16 years old, being a mother in the natural way was not a choice I had from that point. The chemotherapy and resulting hysterectomy put paid to that and it's something I long ago accepted and, if anything, I'm proud of.

It makes me who I am, and my lack of patience with being in a state of indecision or listening to bullshit for very long is born from the inner knowing I have – the understanding that you just never know how long you have or what's around the corner.

That's the point of this section because, *at any given point*, you may be affected by what happens to others around you and by what happens to you. It may not be career-related but can have dramatic and sometimes long-lasting effects on your career and your future life choices.

The older and more experienced we become, the more likely it is that one or more of these developments in the cycle of life will affect us:

○ Becoming pregnant

○ Undergoing IVF or treatment

○ Experiencing a miscarriage

○ Returning from maternity leave

○ Personal ill-health

○ Close family or spouse's ill-health or death

○ Aging parents needing your support

○ Death of a parent, parents or in-laws

○ Divorce

○ Personal redundancy or that of your partner

I've learned from my clients and from my own personal experience that one of the most significant moves you can make for yourself during these times of emotional challenge is to inform those close to you at work. To invite support and help is not a sign of weakness; it is truly a sign of strength and courage.

You're likely to be the first person to help or support

someone who approaches you with these kinds of emotional challenges. You must be prepared to do the same for yourself. Involve others so they can support you, make allowances for you and give you the space or understanding you need to make these challenging and inevitable life developments easier and less stressful to navigate. I encourage you to believe you don't have to handle it all or work it all out by yourself because people want to support and make things easier for you.

I remember a client who went through a gruelling couple of rounds of IVF to try to become pregnant. At no point did she tell her boss or anyone in her team. She put herself under enormous pressure by trying to 'keep calm and carry on' instead of sharing a little about what was going on with her boss so he could understand why she needed flexibility.

I had split up with a long-term partner the weekend before a key meeting with my fiery and, at times, explosive boss. First thing on the Monday morning I told him the headlines of what had happened and said "I'm not my normal robust self at the moment – I want you to know so you can go a little easier on me if I'm not as responsive as usual." It was so interesting. He thanked me for telling him, empathised about how tough it can be splitting up with someone and was much less fiery than he normally was. We both felt better as a result.

It's part of your organisation's responsibility to allow your wider life challenges to be understood and, as far as possible, be accommodated. You don't do yourself or others who work with you justice by trying to put a brave face on it and not involve anyone else. We all have *our* version of this and it's all part of life's rich tapestry and the continuous, unpredictable success cycle of our lives.

SUCCESS

**WHAT WE THINK IT
IT *SHOULD* LOOK LIKE**

**WHAT IT REALLY
DOES LOOK LIKE**

*'The road to success
is always under
construction.'*

~ *LILY TOMLIN*

"We don't have to do it all alone. We were never meant to."

– BRENÉ BROWN

WHAT'S YOUR NEXT MOVE, NOW?

There are many mentions of **additional resources** which I recommend to further support you on your career cycle.

There's a special complimentary pack of resources waiting for you. It includes Your Annual Review & Planning Guide; personal CV guidance; Your Expansion Tree; notes on Your Career Success Cycle – and a couple of extra gems!

Do go and collect these from **www. kaywhite.com/bookresources** – they're put together as a special package for you and that way we can also stay in touch. I send out little eZine every 2 weeks with featured articles relating to career moves and self-confidence. Occasionally I make invitations for you to participate in live and online events and opportunities, all focussed on your career and life success.

You don't have to work it all out by yourself and if you'd ever like to email me with any questions or requests for further support or with your own success stories, here's how. Just email me at **support@kaywhite.com.** You'll always receive a response.

I'm always adding new articles at **www.kaywhite.com** too.

Like you I'm open and listening *and* learning as I go along too. I truly wish you well.

WITH GRACE & GRATITUDE

A myriad of heartfelt Thank You messages in the spirit of gratitude and never wanting to, or being able to, do this all by myself. This book is truly a collaboration and leap of faith for us all. The time felt right for me to just get on and write down what I know to be true.   *There's never been a better time than now.*

Thank you to my ever-supportive husband – *Simon 'Snowy' White*, my lifelong soul mate, playmate and case study. You are my invisible handrail and your love and support are never taken for granted. Thank you for giving me the space and courage to write this book and for your belief in me that I could – and should – do it. Your own tenacity, courage and ability to move through challenges both personal and professional have taught me – and, by default, my clients – so much. I love you.

Thank you to my book-builders – *Kathy Palokoff* and *Helen Slater* my editors, *Janet Lofthouse* for your proofreading skills and to *Erin Stratton*, the designer of this book and of how it's crafted and come together. All your beady eyes, superpowers at what you do, your sound advice and steers were invaluable. I always wanted this book to be a collective and I feel truly lucky to work with you in this way.

Thank you to my Publisher – *Bob Burnham* at Expert Author Publishing in Canada. His first book '101 Reasons Why You Must Write A Book' inspired me to write and trust myself that I could. And still can.

Thank you *to all the many clients* who took time to read and verify *their stories* featured in this book so you could learn from their path. Ladies, you know who you are and I'm *so* very proud of you and grateful to you. Together, we've made something very special which will inspire others to follow in your smart, strategic footsteps. *We as women like to read the instructions and follow maps*!

Thank you *to all the clients not featured here* – your journeys and results helped shaped my experience and confidence to write this book in the first place. We, as women, often think we have to do things and figure things out by ourselves. We don't. Collaboration and connection is in our make-up and this book is all of us doing just that.

Thank you to you, *dear reader*, as you finish this book. Let this book be a place to come to when you have a doubt or wobble or when you know "hey, it's *always* my move" but you want a quick reminder or gentle prod. Take a breath and take the steps and keep going – the rest is unwritten…

WORKS CITED/REFERENCED

Hill, Napoleon (1937) *Think & Grow Rich*
USA: South Beach Books

Robbins, Mel *(2017) The 5 Second Rule*
USA: Post Hill Press

Johnson Dr, Spencer (1998*) Who Moved My Cheese?*
USA: Vermillion

Covey, Steven R (2004*) The 7 Habits of Highly Effective People*:
London: Simon & Schuster

Robinett, Judy (2014) *How To Be A Power Connector*
USA: McGraw Hill Education

Reed, James (2017) *101 Interview Questions You'll Never Fear Again*
UK: Portfolio Penguin

Yates, Martin John (2017) *Great Answers to Tough Interview Questions*
USA: Kogan Page

Cuddy, Amy *(2015) Presence*
USA: Seven Dials

Jeffers, Susan (1987) *Feel The Fear And Do It Anyway*
USA: Vermillion

Smith, Paul (2012) *Lead With A Story*
USA: AMCOM